THE SUGAR
AND THE HUNGER

An Inquiry into the Sugar Regions
of Northeastern Brazil

Robert Linhart

Translated from the French
by John M Floyd

BACK FROM EXILE

On the 1st of April 1964, the Brazilian Army put an end to the hopes for a democratic presidential term of João Goulart with a *coup d'État*. Arrests, executions, torture, departures into exile. Brazil entered into a military dictatorship.

In the North-East of the country, the putsch interrupted that which in all memory remains as *o tempo de Arraes*, the time of Arraes.

The elected governor in the State of Pernambuco at the end of 1962, Miguel Arraes, did not exercise his mandate for more than fourteen months. During this short period, he multiplied the initiatives to try to give birth to forms of popular power and to transform social structures. Arbitration between factory owners and sugar workers, application of workers' rights, refusal to use the police against peasants, organisation of cooperatives, intense alphabetisation and schooling, base assemblies, struggle against corruption.

More than anything else, one measure was etched into the memory of the rural population: a 300% rise in the wages of sugarcane workers. In a few days, all the stores of Recife, the capital of the state, were emptied of their everyday consumables: shoes, radios, chairs, beds, clothes, meat. One bore witness to a rush of agricultural workers for the goods that had been, up until then, inaccessible. This unbelievable and short-lived opulence is still today, by those who experienced it, described as a sort of miracle.

On the evening of the 31st of March 1964, the palace of the State Government of Pernambuco was invaded and occupied by the army. For several hours the military putschists demanded the dismissal of Arraes. He refused. They imprisoned him, first in the military prison of Recife, and then on an island. He passed several weeks in silence and experienced, for a short duration, blindness. After more than one year of detention, he went into exile in Algeria.

Paris, September 14th 1979. An amnesty is proclaimed in Brazil. After fifteen years of exile, Miguel Arraes returns to Pernambuco. I go with him on this journey back.

The plane is late. They put us in an airport lounge—a beige moquette, a garish red ceiling, a falsely relaxing atmosphere. The ancient Governor, a sturdy face, moustache and grey hair, eyes half-closed, was deepseated in a chair, seemingly absent, dreaming.

Around him people were whispering about
the delay and its consequences. The meeting
in Rio upon arrival? The following trip to Crato,
where his mother lives? A certain anxiety
in this prolonged waiting, announcements of
further delays, the comings and goings of
the stewardesses of Varig.

I ask Arraes which, in his opinion, were
the most important measures that he under-
took as governor.

—First of all, I withdrew the police from
social conflicts and increased the salaries of
the agricultural workers. Secondly, during this
period of high inflation, I tried to defend the
real wages of the workers by creating a state
enterprise that sold all staple foods: dried meat,
rice, black beans. They were sold 35% cheaper.
Through this circuit, we managed to take hold
of some 60% of the markets of those products
in eight months. I was democratising credit in
favour of the small-scale property owners and
defending the price of their products. In the
sertão, dominated by local bosses, I could not
do much in just one year of my mandate...

Then Arraes starts to speak about what
one could do now, along Rio São Francisco
and in other regions of the Pernambuco State.
Introducing simple technologies, realising
concrete things that could relieve the Northeastern misery. As if, during all those years
in prison and exile, he had not stopped to

pursue the brutally interrupted mandate in his mind.

Southern and central Brazil was again shaken by strikes and demonstrations. But the North-East, which is the poorest region, did not show any signs of unrest. What did this silence conceal? What were we going to find in the interior?

The amnesty, the moments that stirred Brazilian society, and the relative loosening of state pressure, all presented a chance to inquire into the countryside.

Upon arrival in Recife, I seized the first opportunity that presented itself to go to the interior of the sugar zone. What I experienced there shattered me.

PROLOGUE

You are driving a car down a very decent road. You pass by petrol stations and restaurants. Your radio is playing a Beatles song, or the latest disco hit. On the side of the road men are walking, covered by their straw hats, tools in their hands. You stop. You pick up two or three, to give them a ride. You speak to them. They answer you. They are going to work in the sugar fields. You pose questions about their living conditions. They give you short answers, disjointed phrases. And you understand, as they speak, that they are hungry, their women are hungry, their children are hungry. And if you have the equivalent of 200 French francs in your pocket, that you spend on petrol, food and minor expenses, you learn that this sum is all that their families have at their disposal, their families of five, eight, ten persons, to live (live?) for one month... They get out of your car, thank you, and go on to cross the countryside by foot. You shift gears, the radio speaker announces the latest hit of this or that star. There is, at the end of the landscape, a beautiful church, baroque,

white and yellow. The sugar fields, all green,
quiver on the hills, dense and similar, from
a distance, to the well-kept lawns of golf clubs.
The powerful engine of your Ford swallows
the curves of the road that roll through the
valleys of the *zona da mata*, the old forest.
You are crossing a little village, movie posters
announce *The Sex Nurses* and *The Return of
Frankenstein*. The streets are animated. The
road, again, that takes you far away. For you,
life continues.

I
THE DAY LABOURERS
FROM PRINCESS SERRANA

There is, in the North-East of Brazil, in the State of Pernambuco, a little village that they call 'the Princess Serrana,' the princess of the hills, because it is laid out on three hills and, by night, these three hills, illuminated by the dwellings and streetlights, are visible from afar to beautiful effect.

The Princess Serrana is centrally located in the sugar region, in the middle of the *engenhos* (sugar plantations, where they formerly produced sugar, hence the name, that evokes the machines) and the *usinas* (sugar refineries, the other kind of factories are called *indústrias*).

It is towards this village of the *zona da mata* of the North that we are heading on this Monday, September 17th. We left Recife at nightfall, around five o'clock. In the car, Reynaldo, the student who carries me along, says to me: "The social situation is very, very delicate. There is a really dreadful misery." As he says this I look at the fires of the night on both sides of the road. I think about Manuel da Conçeição, our peasant friend of the State of Maranhão, who, speaking about

these burnt lands, said: "They burn the forest,
the rain blends the ashes with the earth, and
it becomes great, great..." But an agronom explained to me some days ago in Recife that
these fires are destroying the protections against
erosion and threaten the soil of the hills
(and this region is a region of hills). When the
road turns, and a new landscape takes shape
in the night, new fires appear far away.
A sweet smell of sugar enters the car, small
fragments of sugar bark hang in the air and
fly quietly around the illumination of the
headlight. The sugar surrounds us throughout
the night.

Reynaldo points out at a light and fume
on our left: a sugar factory whose owner took
his life fifteen days ago. Family problems, money
problems. A communist daughter who was
recently killed by the police in São Paulo.
He didn't know what to do with his money.
They don't know the exact reasons.

There is a tension between the workers
and peasants of the sugar zone, but there
is also a tension between the sugar patrons,
says Reynaldo. It seems that Delfim Netto
(the Minister of Planning) wants to drive small
sugar refineries to bankruptcy, to leave the
field free for the big enterprises and, certainly,
to the multinationals. This is a part of their
"model" (for Brazil, the great agricultural export
country). They modernised, they mechanised,

they developed the production of fuel based on sugar, and all the "small" manufacturing that doesn't have the means to follow this technological shake-up will be swept away. Others say that they will raise the wages of the sugar workers because Arraes is back.

Arriving. The village at night. Three hills, the lights. A childhood friend of Reynaldo speaks to us, reluctantly, about the rumours of a strike in the sugar fields. The block of brothels, all along a street of firmly packed earth. Red lights, disco music. There are televisions everywhere, even in the most miserable rooms, the emptiest, open to the street. Reynaldo: "I went to one of these brothels at the age of nine. Here, it's very 'macho', one must prove one's manhood. There are some very young prostitutes, ten, twelve years old."

People are ambling about the village square, dominated by a sloping garden, into the late hours, and we are also walking. Cards and alcohol are the main distractions. There are many alcoholics in this town.

Tuesday morning, early, in a sugar field.

First of all, the visit to the *bodega*, the farm store where the workers buy their vital commodities and go into debt. A poor grocer in a hut. Some workers, some children—almost all of them carrying the little scythe of the sugar cutters—, some dogs. A woman behind the counter. The smell of sugar, dust, spices. Everyone is in debt, and the money from the salaries never leaves the farm. "It is more expensive here than in the city, but the people here can't go to the city to buy things." (The city, Princess Serrana, is 5 kilometres from here.)

—And if people get sick? we ask.

Laughter.

—Nothing. Sickness, it is God that makes it grow, like potatoes. And an old man, echoing, with a rasping voice, shouts:

—Sickness? *Nada. Nada. Nada.* (Nothing. Nothing. Nothing.)

The workers say that they have started to talk about a strike in the city. There will be a gathering this Sunday to decide.

—The strike of the poor, it's to gain just
a little more. But we speak about a lot more.
Even one hundred, one hundred and ten
cruzeiros a day (fifteen francs).

Exit from the *bodega*. Crossing the sugar fields. A *feitor* (foreman): red shirt, a portable scale, a notebook in his hand. He keeps watch on four or five workers, scattered among the sugarcanes, cutting and gathering bundles. We ask to see his notebook. He shows it to us: here are the names, and on the opposite page, the daily production. The page from the day before: together, it varies between 500 and 1500 kilos each day.

—2250 on this line: how come?

—It's a guy who comes with his granddaughter.

—And here, 150: why so little?

—It's a six-year-old child: that is how much he does a day (150 kilos of canes; the salary is on output, the child earned 8 cruzeiros, about a franc.)

"Around five o'clock," says the *feitor*, "we count, on the spot." He points towards two Black men who are cutting cane just next to us. "These two over there are *da rua* (from the town)." Both men stop working and one of them answers our questions::

—I get up at four in the morning to start
here at six. I am *volante*: I work one day here,
one day there.

—Why are you leaving the city to come
work here? Can't you find any other work?

—*Tem nada* (there is none), he says with
a disgusted pout.

He lights a cigarette and says nothing.
The *feitor* shows us the bundle that he is tying
together: "If he does a hundred like this,
he will have his 1500 kilos."

We move away and they continue to cut.
Slow steps. Tropical mugginess. This drawling
way to speak Brazilian. We feel an interior exhaustion. In front of us, close to the sugarcane
that they are cutting, a zone of burnt land.
On the trail, at the foot of the hill, a blue truck
is loading four men—the quiver of cane bundles.
A lapping of a stream in the midst of the burnt
earth. The smell of ashes. The wind carries
these flakes of ash that enter everywhere, in
the houses, the bedrooms. The sound of voices
from afar in the canes, and of the cane that is
being cut. In the background of the landscape,
the *casa grande* (the master's house), surrounded
by palm trees, a whiteness almost concealed
from the gaze. All around us, a horizon of hills.
And in this mugginess, these feeble sounds,
this sweltering valley, always, always a strong
sensation of exhaustion.

THREE
DAY LABOURERS

We leave by car for the city.

Three *caboclos* (*Caboclo*, originally to describe a mixed-race indigenous person, used by colloquial extension to denote a miserable peasant) are walking along the trail. We pick them up. They are agricultural workers.

—What do you call it, asks Reynolds, *boias frias* or *volantes*? (There are many notions in Brazil to designate day labourers that walk from one place to another: *boias frias*—cold lunch-boxes, *volantes, clandestinos...*)

—We don't know the word *boias frias*. They call us *volantes*. They laugh as they specify this point of terminology.

—How many are you in this town?

—Five thousand, says one.

—Many more, says another.

—Every day there are thirty trucks going in different directions, specifies the third.

One of them is sweating heavily. Without us asking him, he says, in one stroke: "I have been certified insane. They have interned me four times in the asylum. Six months each time." ("They say asylum, but it is a psychiatric

prison," whispers Reynaldo.) "But I am not
a fool. I have been working too much. It is
a weakness. It is hunger. I am not a fool."
    —Are you not organised? asks Reynaldo.
    —No.
    —You have to organise.
    —*Sim senhor.* (Yes sir.)
    —You are all being exploited.
    —*Sim senhor.*
    The car speeds on along the trail of
earth, the colour of ochre, between two dense
walls of cane, on aisles in banana and *caju*
plantations.
    We ask the day labourers if they
remember 1964, before the *coup d'État.*
    —Yes, at that time the salaries were rising.
    —What do you think about the return
of Miguel Arraes?
    —It is the best thing that could happen.

AT THE BARBER

In the city, the vividness of a market town.
With its nerve centres: cafés, public gardens.
The barber is one of these centres. We pose
a question about the *boias frias* (Reynaldo is
still designating them as such, as one does in
the majority of the country and in the politicised milieus).

   —In the morning, at five, there is a big
gathering of *boias frias* going to work, close to
the cattle park. Go see them, you will see many
children, ten years or younger. The father goes
with three children. These trucks are dangerous. There are many accidents, people get killed,
disabled. Yesterday a child, disabled after one
of these accidents, came here to beg. A truck
sometimes carries a hundred people, and they
drive like fools.

    A young man sitting in a chair mimics
the foolish driving of the day labourers' trucks.
The barber, small and with a moustache, gives
his explanation while he is shaving a client laid
as if he were on a surgeon's table, and follows
with an anxious look at the often brutal progression of the razor. The client holds a bank

report in his hand. He must be employed in the bank next door.

The barbershop is blue, furnished with yellow chairs, cluttered with things and people. Photographs of football teams hang on the walls. A sign, at the exterior: 'Salon Figaro.' It is indeed carrying its name well: here one discusses politics, social problems, journalism (a right-wing guy is going to launch a new local radio station and everyone is trying to determine its possible reach).

We would follow the recommendation of the barber: the next day, at dawn, we were among the *boias frias* when the trucks were departing.

That very same afternoon we visited the building of the future local radio (a selfsatisfied tour given by the promoter, a young man with dirty blond hair, the son of a latifundist, who had invited the military police brass band for the opening), the hospital (they spoke to us about the maladies that are tormenting the population of the region, the Chagas disease, spread by a tree parasite that touches everyone in the rural areas because the people, too poor to buy beds or straw mattresses, sleep on the soil: in a small neighbouring village 90% of the peasants are effected—and affected by hunger, the primary illness), a sugar factory (noise, warmth, smoke, steam—the book of José Lopes, on the work in sugar refineries,

is called *The Steam of the Devil*, and the title
of this book, drawn from an interview with
a sugar worker, immediately gets to your throat—
the workers, working in two teams, twelve
hours each, get paid 664 cruzeiros, less than
one hundred francs per week).

Toward five o'clock in the evening, we are searching for the union of agricultural workers in the streets of the lower city, not far from the brothels. It is closed, but they send us to someone from the union—a greenhouse, close to the bridge. The wife shows us in. Cement floor, greenish walls. A big television set. On the walls there are pious images, a photo of Paul VI, another of President Médici ("the most repressive," whispers Reynaldo), a municipal deputy diploma of Arena (the governing party). To the right, a room with cribs. Behind, another room where one distinguishes a big red refrigerator.

A man enters, he finishes buttoning up his shirt. He has a round head, a lacklustre, little, greasy face. He looks like a bookkeeper. A Portuguese-looking type (his wife is more native).

He is not the head of the union he says, only its employee, responsible for the bureau work. He has worked for the union for more than fifteen years and can explain everything to us.

—The union was founded in 1962, by
the Church. It was a Jesuit priest, now dead.
A Dutchman... No, wait, it was... A Pole. But
he spoke good Portuguese—with an accent.
He was *bem vermelho*, very red. (I am confusing
the sense of the adjective: it is not about political engagement, as we will see, but without doubt about a physical trait, or an idea of
energy.) This Father was the Bishop's assistant.
He invited a farmer to join forces, and together
they founded the union.

—Was it a left-wing Father?

—Oh no! The union was founded by the
Church in order to fight the peasant leagues
of Julião that were bringing disorder, demonstrations, and wanted to start a revolution. Besides,
one week before the *coup d'État* the peasant
league threatened to bring a hundred people
and violently destroy the union (a retrospective
fear reached his face as he invoked this event
taking place fifteen years ago).

—What happened to the leaders of
the peasant league?

—The president of the league died in
misery in Olinda. He was illiterate. He became
a beggar there, in Recife. Nobody knows where
the second leader disappeared to. No one
has seen him since. The treasurer continued
to agitate. He was put in prison in 1964,
and again in 1968. In sum, he spent nine years
in prison. He has just been given amnesty.

He is light-skinned and mixed-race. Literate.
(The employee speaks of these hunted-down
peasant leaders like the slave-owners used to
speak of revolting slaves one hundred years
ago: "Black," "bright," "illiterate," "literate,"
a few physical traits—"big," "medium"...)

—What does the work of the union
consist of?

—Judicial assistance to agricultural
workers and medical aid.

—How many members does the union have?

—In our *município*, 7452 members.

—And how many agricultural workers are
there in the same area?

—About twenty thousand now. In 1970,
it was about fourteen thousand.

—Is everyone included in this number,
also the *boias frias*?

—Yes. Moreover, most of the agricultural
workers live in the city now. If you are going
to the square tomorrow, where the trucks pick
them up, at four thirty or five o'clock, you
will see them leave. As there is no assistance
in the countryside, they go *pra rua* (in the
street, the city). There, in the countryside,
there is no soil to cultivate anymore, and no
education. This departure in trucks, in the
morning, is impressive. One sees children at
the age of twelve or less go to harvest canes.
Many children become disabled through the
work, cutting their hands, fingers. And they

can't do anything in court, since children under
thirteen aren't allowed to work... Among
the *boias frias*, if there are ten children, the girls
wear pants and the boys a shirt. That's all.
There is nothing, nothing. We have received
an order from Recife to make an inquiry into
the salaries and the work, because they speak
about a strike.

—Who?

—The unions. The unions want to show
that they are on the side of the workers.
So they told the journals that they would
go on strike. Meetings between the owners,
unions and deputies of the Ministry of
Labour have already started. But the situation for a strike is very bad. The workers
have no soil, nothing to keep up. For there
to be a strike, 50% of the workers must agree
to it.

We try to clarify the modalities of this
50%, but it remains confusing. One thing, at
least, becomes clear when the union employee
makes his explanations: the number of seven
thousand members is heavily inflated.

—Out of seven thousand, not even four
thousand pay the union fee. If there were
seven thousand paying members, this would
be the biggest union in the region. But anyway,
this union is very good.

—What did you do before working for
the union?

—I was a seminarian, an aspiring Salesian.
For a long time I did all kinds of work for the
Church, except the sacraments. I am still very
attached to the Church. I am a member of the
society of Saint-Vincent-de-Paul (he shows us
a book that contains the rules of the society,
in a Brazilian edition). There are many
Vincentists here.

We ask him about his projects, how he conceives of his future. He wants to quit the union.
He would like to teach law. He is registered
at the "University" in a little town nearby (it is
not the university, but the regional education
centre, specifies Reynaldo): he has started
to study social science. How old is he? Thirty-
three. What does he think about the union
now? What were the union's failings?

—The leaders of the union aren't genuine.
They stay above it all, they don't explain
the workers' rights to them.

—Is the union political?

—The union is neutral.

—And you? (Reynaldo points to the municipal deputy diploma of ARENA that hangs
on the wall.)

—I was politically organised in ARENA.
I started in 1968: a political colleague and
photographer dragged me into it. I was *vereador*
(locally elected). But I want to drop it. Politics
is inhuman. It's all yes or all no. I want to leave
that. (A disgusted pout.)

—What do people here say about the
political process, about the return of Arraes,
all that?

—The workers don't speak. After the
massacres, the persecutions; they don't speak.

I think: to him, certainly not.
But they speak.

—Julião's return?

—The peasants don't want to hear about
that. The union and the Church have shown
them that their ideas were false. What is
needed is only social assistance. He, Julião,
wanted to steal from others, he wanted
the violence.

—And Arraes?

—In his time, it's true, the salary was higher...
But people don't speak about politics. I don't
speak about politics outside. I vote for people,
not for parties. I voted against Arraes, Julião,
Jango (Goulart), because they were troubled
times. If they come back, that's okay. But
if they have influence on the institutions? No!
All they have to do is to withdraw and no
longer do politics. After the "revolution" they
all went abroad, but the poor remained here.
The first leader of the union went to prison, he
was tortured ...

Silence.

—I have always been occupied with others.
Now I want to live for myself.

—You are very appalled? ask Reynaldo.

—Yes.

At this moment of the discussion,
a scene erupts at the other end of the room.
Fascinated, I can't turn my eyes away. The wife
of the employee is quite young, her face has
indigenous traits, and she is sitting on a divan
and has, up until now, been listening without
saying a word, just holding her baby, about
ten months old, in her arms.

The child starts to cry. Immediately
the mother turns to the wall, where an enormous portrait of Christ crowned with thorns is
hanging, and she holds her baby in the direction of the image, and she shakes it and repeats
like a litany: *Papai do céu! Papai do céu! Papai
do céu!* (Heavenly Father! Heavenly Father!)
The child stops crying.

The employee says that he had been
"used as an intervention" by the government
in a nearby little village to replace the union
leadership that "had problems," and Reynaldo
remarks to me the extent to which this means
that he's allied to the dictatorship.

The child starts to cry again. The jolts
and the incantation in front of the image of
the thorn-crowned also starts again. *Papai
do céu! Papai do céu!* At every moaning or
movement of the child: *Papai do céu!* During
this ritual, the face of the mother takes
a blissful, almost ecstatic air: a broad smile,
bulging eyes. The child smiles vaguely as it

looks at the pious image and during the bumps, cries a little. Finally, a teat and the *Papai do ceu* calm him definitively. He is huddled up in his pants, swollen by swaddling cloths, and falls silent.

We speak about the "revolution" of 1964 (the military coup). This maintained order, says the employee, and that is what's most important. But, on the other hand, it didn't work out well because of the commerce: the workers gained much but couldn't buy anything. (He wants to say that the nominal wages were rising, but the inflation was such that the real wages were falling to an extremely low level. All this was communicated in a confusing fashion, with an expression of anxiety.)

We left and outside the door was the cold evening air: streets of trampled earth, houses in all colours—rose, green, yellow, ochre, blue...

We exchanged our impressions of the demoralisation of the ARENIST, enrolled by the right in the official agricultural union before he was twenty, today bitter and conscious of his failure. There is no one here to be found, in the countryside in the North-East, that defends the politics of the dictatorship of the past fifteen years—so obvious is the catastrophic deterioration of living conditions.

We also speak about the extraordinary organisational force of the Church, in both one sense and the other.

—The right of the Church is very dynamic,
one must not forget, says Reynaldo to me.

We go back to sleep in the house of a plantation master, the owner of which Reynaldo knows. A shadow, standing against a pillar, is guarding the house. "Everything okay?" asks Reynaldo. "Everything's okay," answers the shadow. He remains there the entire night. We pass him again in the morning. All these invisible eyes, in the shadows of the powerful, that are waiting for the miracle of a word, a favour, a gaze. A terrible Brazil...

In the night, a sudden burst traverses the chamber and wakes me up. A bat flies, panic-stricken, from one corner of the room to the other, before hiding under the beams of the ceiling. I am reminded of a newspaper article I read recently, about an attack carried out by multiple rabid vampire bats that wounded several inhabitants. This idea keeps me awake in the great silence of the night. When dawn approaches, the noise of the countryside life—cockerels, dogs, birds and even a far away radio—delivers me.

Wednesday, four in the morning. We leave in the night towards the still illuminated Princess Serrana to be present for the departure of the *boias frias*. It happens here, in this vague junction of streets and roads, while on the foot of the hill the lights flicker off as the day rises, a fruit market is set up. Some trucks are already waiting, with the beginning of a cargo of day labourers scattered in shells, pressed against the side rail, sitting aboard or standing in the middle. Ripped trousers and shirts, bags, old tied-up sacks, all the miserable parapher-nalia rather belonging to the vagabond than the worker.

Men and children flock on foot in the converging streets. Stooping and solitary shadows: no one arrives in a group, no one speaks. The silence of this crowd is impressive.

Here is a blue and green truck covered in pious images and portraits of Christ in the front and rear (all the trucks are decorated in this way). Discussion with the workers. This man quit the farm where he was living one year ago to come live in the city. Now he goes back every morning. It is the farm of a sugar factory, and about forty workers are employed there. There aren't so many workers in the truck. We ask why. A man answers us. He sports a moustache and a cap, he has wellingtons. He speaks fast, in a very nervous manner, shouting some words spasmodically: "When it is easy to earn money, they come. When it is not, no." The salary? A man in blue: "There are some that pay fifty, fifty–five cruzeiros for each *quadra* (square with a side of twenty-two metres) to clear."

—And the cane cutting?

—Sixty cruzeiros each for the people outside of the farm, fifty-five for those inside.

—Why this difference?

—To attract the people outside.

—And those inside, don't they complain about the difference?

—If they complain, they send them out.

The ferocity of the sugar owners has had absurd consequences, including for themselves. By appropriating all the individual parcels of subsistence crops—*roças*—and thus causing an enormous exodus that has thrown the rural workers out of the land and into the slums and the most miserable quarters of the city, they have at the same time created the conditions for a terrible extension of the hunger, and rendered unstable and insecure their own labour. Henceforth they themselves cannot foresee

the exact number of sugarcane cutters that
they will have on their own plantations. Everyone is saying that the function of exploitation
has become more difficult since before.

—What is the minimum salary?

—Nobody knows.

—It is impossible to do more than a *quadra*,
fifty cruzeiros a day (seven francs).

—Fifty cruzeiros, enough to die of hunger,
says a worker that looks like a pirate.

—Are you better off now when you're
coming *pra rua*, from the city? Or is it worse?

—The farm was worse than the street.
The boss forced us to work the entire week,
from Sunday to Sunday.

—Yes, but now, after working five days
a week, we get 250 cruzeiros (thirty-five
francs). How do you feed a family with that?
It's impossible!

—And when the sugar harvest stops, what
do you do?

—We don't do anything, there is nothing.
You go one day there, another day there...

—During the sugar season (eight months,
from September to May) the trucks come to pick
us up in the city. But afterwards, nothing. We
are *no meio do mundo*. Lost in the middle of the
world. (He who says this has a sympathetic and
sad expression, curly hair and a moustache,
an old grey shirt. He thinks that it was better
na mata, in the countryside, than here, *na rua*.)

On the farm we could do some cultivation for ourselves.

—Here it's ten thousand times as hard, says an old man, we are almost always hungry.

—How many of you leave in this way each day?

—Eight thousand, maybe.

Next to the one that gives us the number is a child.

—How old is he?

—Fifteen. (He looks twelve.)

—For how long has he been working here?

—For three years. There are many small children that can't lift their tools, but whose fathers oblige them to work.

—Do you have unions?

—No.

—Why?

Silence. And then a voice: "Because we cannot pay." He who has a sympathetic face pushed into a grey shirt says: "I have a card and I cannot pay." He who speaks spasmodically: "And the union doesn't do anything. Before 1964 it was better. We didn't earn much but the products were cheaper."

—What do you eat?

—Flour, *feijão* (black beans).

—Meat?

—If you speak about meat, you go to prison.

—Are there any strikes?

—No. Strikes, that means the baton, prison...

—What do you think about the return
of Arraes?

—Many are afraid of violence.

—He could help raise wages, says another.

—*Nos estamos vivos e esperamos.* We are
alive and have hope.

Exactly at the moment when the worker
says this phrase, the truck starts up. The
hour is twenty past six. Music from afar,
a shapeless samba, reaches us from the poor
houses close to the market, at the foot of
one of the hills.

We move closer to another truck that is
waiting with its human cargo. Having barely
asked a question, a very agitated person shoots
out from the cabin—short haircut, glasses, grey
shirt, fifty-something, an authoritarian appearance: "Who are you? What are you doing?
What do you want?" I say that I am a French
journalist, that I am reporting on the North-
East. This seems to calm him. He is the farmer
of four plantations, 645 hectares in total.
What does he think about the situation here?
He enters into a farcical discussion: "It is good.
The only thing is that they don't have money:
do you? Nobody agitates, we are all brothers.
It is magnificent. There are no strikes, nothing!
Everybody is satisfied. The only problem is
that there is no money." The workers crammed
together in the car listen to him as he churns

out his tirade. Some of them laugh out of obsequiousness. Nobody makes any comment. Afterwards, he returns to the cab and the truck drives off straight away.

A third truck, packed. Black men, *caboclos*, children. We enter the car to speak more easily. The workers of this plantation earn fifty-seven cruzeiros per tonne, and they gather about a tonne each day. They all live in the city. "Before" most of them lived in the plantation. But the patron has taken all, *roças*, individual parcels, and told them to leave. Are they members of the union? Only one, the others, no. A toothless Black man shouts: "I earn three hundred cruzeiros a week! I work the whole week to buy a sardine! Where do I get the money to pay a union?" An old man, with white hair, who is carrying a calabash: "On top of that, the union doesn't help." Another: "Even medical assistance is rare." We step down from the car. A guy sitting in the cabin of the truck, with a cowboy hat, questions us in a hostile manner: "What is this about?" "French journalist?" He shrugs his shoulders and gives the signal to depart. I tell myself that all could easily become violent at the least suspicion of agitation, that there must be guns in the cars, henchmen ready to intervene. The police are not far away. I have seen the municipal prison in a little nearby city, in a street that goes up:

a public cage, with a man locked up. Behind the drowsy routine of this departure in the dusk, one perceives a terrible lurking violence.

Meanwhile, the trucks that we left are moving away, a child of eight or nine years, whose skinny shoulders come out of the torn-up t-shirt, is clinging to a bin with his eyes fixed upon us. His gaze pierces me.

THE UNION
OF AGRICULTURAL WORKERS

The place is modest: several rooms, almost all empty, leading into each other, with a big meeting room at the far end.

In a narrow corridor, where we are waiting for the union president, who will arrive at seven-thirty, a man waits with us. He wears the straw hat of the sugarcane cutters and worn-out sandals. He has a gentle demeanour, a sad smile. He explains his presence to someone passing by (there is movement, the day is beginning). Yesterday his son died, he was one month and six days old. He would like a coffin. He is a member of the union: could the union buy a coffin for the baby? No, the union won't pay, says the treasurer, passing through a door standing ajar. When a worker dies, the union can pay for a coffin. But not when a child dies. He should go to the town council. How did he die? we ask the peasant.

—The child was *doentinho*, a little sick, he had diarrhoea. We took him to the hospital on Saturday, he stayed there for a day and then they handed him back.

—Was he feeling better?

—No, he was still sick... Yesterday I went away to work. When I came back, the child was dead.

—How many children do you have?

—Six living children, six dead.

—At what age did they die?

—Six months, one year, around that age...

The people around us, in the corridor, agree: "One out of two children die, that's generally how it goes."

The president of the union arrives and invites us into his little office. The door remains open and the people in the corridor gather at the entrance to listen to the conversation. The president looks native, his skin is deep brown. He wears a denim hat.

We say to him that we would like to get an idea of the evolution of the working conditions since the *coup d'État* of 1964. How was it before, and how has it become?

—Good. The president of the union makes us an accurate account. He begins with the salaries. In 1963-1964 the salaries were reasonable: 503 cruzeiros a day (since then there has been a change of currency and new cruzeiros). The salary was based on a workday and not on a tonne or a piece, as it is today.

—What was the piece (*tarefa*) for a day?

—One hundred fifty bundles of twenty canes. Each bundle weighed around five kilos, about 750 kilos in total. For the cut. And for

the clearance of the *mata*, one had to make
a *quadra*. The area of the *quadra* depends upon
the type of *mata* (undulating or not), but this
is roughly twenty-two square metres.

—How long was the workday?

—This depended on the conditions. If
everything worked out well, one could do it
in three hours. On average, it took five or six
hours to do it.

—Were there any days off?

—Some farms gave Sundays off.

—What happened after 1964?

—The wages rose, but in reality, given
the inflation, the purchasing power diminished.
Above all, they gave up the *tabelas* (the general
norms and rates for the cutting and the clearance) and the definition of the salaries and
pieces fell *a vontade dos empresarios*, at the
discretion of the employers. They profited
from it by augmenting the pieces little by little.
From 1964 up until now they have doubled:
when it formerly was necessary to make 750
kilos, one must now make 1500.

—Let us try to compare the salaries from
1964 to those today.

As the money has changed and there has
been enormous inflation, the comparison is
difficult. We are using basic goods as a bench-
mark both now and then—*feijão*, sugar, salt,
kerosene, meat. Reynaldo made an example
of a budget in 1964 and one now. One clearly

noticed a decline in purchasing power.
The peasant coming to ask for a coffin for his
child agrees: "We bought more at that time
and, above all, everybody cultivated *roças*,
individual parcels."

In the corridor, peasants were flocked
with membership forms and identity papers—
obligatory presentations. There are now a lot
of people in the little office of the president.
The floor is made of cement, the walls are
painted green. A sort of cellar window gives
a little light, but protects against the exterior
heat. One hears the sound of voices on
the streets.

The president of the union says: "They
have done away with the *roças* everywhere and
put canes in their place." Everyone confirms this.

Reynaldo based the calculations on data
given by the president: Before, a family earned
600 cruzeiros a week, which is the minimum
to be able to eat (*minimissimo*). Today, a family
earns about 380 cruzeiros a week—two equivalent sums of money, counted according to
the price of commodities. In this way, the salary
since 1964 has been divided in two, and the daily
production for each man multiplied by two.

—Do the people take that into account?
asks Reynaldo.

The president raises his head:
"Everybody knows that. It's like that everywhere in the cane region."

—Has the area of the cane increased?

—Yes, by more than 60%.

—And for the other crops?

—They have disappeared from the region. The cane has overrun everything.

The father of the dead child exemplifies this with his own case: before, he had one *roça* (oh, a little *roça*, about one or two *quadras*, around twenty or forty square metres) and sometimes he even managed to sell the surplus, when there was one. Now it is over, he needs to buy everything.

—Where does the food come from now?

—From the State of Paraiba, the State of Bahia, from Rio Grande do Norte, from Ceará. (And of course, the price of the transport contributes to the price of essential food products.)

Before 1964 the farm where the president of the union worked produced five thousand tonnes of cane. Last year it produced sixteen thousand. "They have increased the area by taking everyone's *roças*."

—Did the peasants protest?

—Some came to see the union, but there was nothing that could be done. The patron put a fence around the *roça*, said that it was over and didn't give anything in exchange. That was everything.

—Were there any strikes?

—Before 1964 there were strikes. Since 1964, none.

—We have been told that they are starting to speak about strikes again. Will there be strikes here?

—There is a collective campaign to raise wages. If the "men" (the owners) don't agree, there might be a strike.

—What are the demands?

—An 100% increase of the wage and a return to the *tabela* system for the clearance and cutting.

The president says that the conditions of the agricultural workers are more severe now that 80% of them live in the city (and it is like this in the entire sugarcane region). Only 20% still live in the *mata*, in the countryside. Almost everyone needs work trucks to get to work and, when the season is over, it is very difficult to find work.

—What do they say about the return of Arraes?

—They are illiterate. They speak little, but they speak about it.

—And you, what do you think?

—I think his return is normal.

—The people, are they frightened?

—The poor class, no. Everyone is pleased. They think that things will change, become like before. I think that the union will work more because, with the return of Arraes, the workers will turn to the union.

—Does the union have any political links?

—No. Besides, it is against the law.

—And do you have relations with the Church?

—Me personally? I go to mass and back again, that's all.

—The *boias frias*, do they have the right to join the union?

—Yes, but they don't, because they can't pay. The fee is thirty-three cruzeiros (five francs) a month. On the last day of every month, the *bodega* (the plantation canteen) takes the money directly to pay the union for those that are inscribed. The workers are in difficulty in the last week of the month.

—Among the twenty thousand or twenty-five thousand agricultural workers of the *municipio*, how many are literate?

—About 90% are illiterate. The people of the government give other numbers, but that is the truth. There is an easy way to verify the large proportion of illiterates, it is sufficient to look at the number of voters. (The illiterates don't have the right to vote: this excludes the majority of agricultural workers from elections.)

Somebody goes to get documents: out of sixty thousand inhabitants, there were, in 1977, 10 938 voters in the city.

—What is the role of the union?

—During the fifteen years that followed 1964, the union was dead and gone. Now, with

this "opening," there are possibilities. Up
until now, it has been impossible to speak
about strikes. I can now speak about strikes.
The work will be better, one will have the
chance to do other things, not only occasional
medical assistance.

—What do you mean when you say
"opening"?

—It is an amnesty. But we started to see
a change in 1974, and it has become clear since
the end of 1977 and the beginning of 1978. Our
federation of agricultural workers has begun
meeting, and there have been contacts with
other states. In May 1979, we held a national
congress for agricultural workers in Brasília.
We discussed a lot...

This new language of the people in charge
of agricultural union activity—initially *pelegos*,
yellow unions, institutionalised by the dictatorship and kept in the role of social and medical
assistance—we heard it here and there in
Pernambuco. They say that things must change,
that the misery is too extensive, that one
has to prepare for a strike—sometimes even
to prepare effectively. Is this union activity
evolving towards one of class struggle, or is it
just jettisoning ballast to keep afloat? One
thing is sure: the defence of the *status quo* is
in full flight and nobody wants to appear
as a partisan for the established order. But the
positions vary according to place and

people–here the presence of a *padre*, elsewhere the traces of an ancient peasant league. Without a doubt, one should not take literally all the certainties of these speeches. People that–in this Brazil of the autumn of 1979–speak up against the dictatorship, the hunger and the misery are legion. But, those who take action are far fewer. The opinions are divided when it comes to the union of Princess Serrana: "This union, even if it isn't *pelego*, doesn't fight much," says a lawyer for the agricultural workers union that we meet some days later in the southern parts of the state, the flattest parts with the largest sugar plantations. But I know that there are also rivalries and personal conflicts that the tensions in civil society fuel. And the starving masses, in the name of which they express themselves, still speak so little...

We went to see the owners of a sugar factory that Reynaldo knows. They received us on the veranda of their white, colonial-style residence from where one has a view of the factory, which spit out its smoke on the other side of a little river, and the workers' houses, all in line, far away on the hills. The *casa grande* (master's house) and the *senzalas* (house of the slaves) have been kept as they were during the time of slavery.

The business manager, son-in-law of the owner, gave us a detailed explanation of the difficulties that the owners of sugar factories in the North-East face: the world commodity price of sugar is very low (three hundred dollars per tonne, compared to 1500 at the beginning of the 1970s), and the stocks too high; all the operations are in the hands of big international *traders*, essentially Americans, that operate on the stock exchange of sugar in London; and the North-East is very dependent on exportation: 70% of the production is exported, even though the region doesn't provide more than half of the sugar produced in Brazil. But there is no local purchasing power; the majority of the terrain is too uneven to lend itself to mechanisation, something that accentuates the difference in production costs in comparison with the São Paolo region, which is much more competitive.

A detail. We are underway evaluating the sugar production of Pernambuco and Alagoas. "Forty-two million packets, sixty kilos each," says the manager, while he swings back in his rocking chair. "But, from this harvest onwards, we will change the unit. We will reduce the weight to fifty kilos, since people are too weak to transport them. Ah, before it was something else! (During the time of slavery.) The men were sturdy and carried sacks that weighed eighty kilos."

This remark engraved itself in my mind, and I lost track of his exposition. Below, workers of the second group entered the factory in small groups. It will be two in the afternoon, they have twelve hours of work ahead in "the steam of the devil."

In the middle of the day, on the way to Recife,
the landscape fully opens out into hills, quive-
ring green: canes, everywhere canes. Here
and there deep brown burned lands. More
rarely, the remainder of tropical forests or
a red hole of fertile soil, cut up by the way.
While driving, Reynaldo tensely read a poem
by Ferreira Gullar that he knows by heart,
'A *bomba suja*' ('The Dirty Bomb'):

"I introduce in poetry / The word diarrhoea... / He who speaks about flowers does not
speak about everything... / If there are no real
words... / The poet becomes speechless / The
diarrhoea / Is an arm that wounds and kills. /
That kills more than the knife, / More than the
rifle bullets / Men, women and children / From
the interior of Brazil... / It is like a D-bomb /
That explodes in the interior of man / With
the slow onset / The setting fire of hunger... /
A bomb placed inside him / By centuries of
hunger / And that explodes in diarrhoea /
In the body of he who does not eat. / It is not
a clean bomb: / It is a filthy and limp bomb /
That without a sound / Eliminates millions

of children / One ends up asking / Who has placed this bomb here / In the heart of this man / Who steals from this man / The cereals that he plants... / It is he who transforms the coffee into dollars / And the rice into hunger..."

The end of the poem speaks about the moment when the weapon of hunger gives way to the weapon of hope.

Recife. Professor Nelson Chaves, a famous nutritionist, is an old man. He works at the Maternal-Infant Institute of the hospital of Pernambuco and lives in an apartment of unusual modesty, cluttered with books, documents and statistics—all concerning one unique theme: "malnutrition." The hunger. This is what he says:

"Starvation is the most important disease we treat in this hospital. 70% of the children of the State of Pernambuco suffer from malnutrition. The situation here is worse than in the *sertão* (the semi-desert region situated higher up in the north, known as a zone of drought and famine, but where the farming practices maintain a dietary diversity, and where the demography is less dense). Worse than before.

The situation was better during the colonial period. The slaves received a proper diet because the slave-owners wanted to maintain their workforce. Later, the progression of hunger in the plantation economy was curbed as long as there were the *roças*. But with the big factories and the monoculture of sugar for export, the scourge of nutritional monotony engulfed the population. Now we see cane all the way into the city and the peasants don't eat anything other than black beans, cassava, and, exceptionally, dried meat. No fish, no milk, no vitamins.

Malnutrition during the embryonal life and the eighteen first months of the baby's life leads to permanent mental disabilities: the baby lacks up to 60% of the necessary brain neurons and this destruction is beyond remedy. Another consequence: the average height decreases. We are heading towards a generation of dwarfs."

(Nutritional monotony: one can die slowly, with a stomach full of poor food simulacra, the vital forces unable to build up again. A hunger without protruding ribs and emaciated limbs, but one that wears down and destroys just as implacably...)

"Two months ago I proposed an emergency plan to fight starvation in the State of Pernambuco. It is necessary to restore food production, reconstitute subsistence crops and poultry farms. It is equally necessary to do something against the boilers of the sugar factories that kill the fish in the rivers by discharging hot water. Up until now, I have had no answers."

Professor Chaves is very pessimistic. Hunger is spreading all over the world, including in the US (he cites a Pan-American medical journal). What to do against this rage of destruction that the species pursues against itself, and leads it to destroy the most profound natural equilibriums? Here, the mechanism of the extension of sugar, on which the entire economy of a region relies, is also that of the extension of hunger.

The pessimistic forecasts of Professor Chaves echoes those I heard from a Brazilian engineer I met in Paris just before I departed:

"The day they installed the first separate pumps for fuel drawn from sugarcane alcohol, they sentenced the populations of the North-East to an ever-worsening situation. As long as they limited themselves to adding a small proportion of sugarcane alcohol (14%) to the petrol, they didn't need to change the motors: they could remain in a temporary situation, and change politics. From now on they need special motors. Volkswagen already produces them, others will follow. The 'third pump' meant an important conversion of the auto industry, investments. No question of going back. Do you understand what this means? The condition for the cost of this new fuel not to be prohibitive, is that they keep the cane workers wages on a level of misery. Up until now those agricultural workers only had a class of declining landowners against them, but now they also have the powerful multinational companies of the auto industry. The sugar will devour new areas of the earth, eliminating that which remains of the subsistence crops. The hunger in the North-East will make the cars go around in the whole country."

When he said this final phrase, he had an expression of disgust.

II
ACCOUNTANCY

A dot that sticks out on the vast Brazilian triangle, in the region closest to Europe. The State of Pernambuco appears so, a long rectangle from the coast to the interior of the North-East. And it is actually here that the Portuguese colonisers installed one of the first canals through which the wealth of Brazil would be drained, throughout the centuries, like a haemorrhage. Sugar first of all.

Three geographical zones order the distribution of culture and men in this rectangle that stretches over more than six hundred kilometres. The coastal strip, a muggy region of about sixty kilometres: this is the *zona da mata*, the old Atlantic forest, today almost cleared and covered with sugar plantations. More to the West one enters the *agreste*, a transitory soil, poorly watered, where small crops subsist. Finally, one is led into the *sertão*, arid of drought and restless wandering, home since time immemorial of great fears, prophecies and rebellions.

From one zone to another and within each zone, men and cultures are in perpetual movement.

The coastal strip itself is divided, approximately according to a line that passes through the capital of the state. In the north of Recife, the *zona da mata norte*, a hilly region occupied by medium-sized sugar plantations. In the south, the *zona da mata sul*, flatter, cut up in very large domains. This southern part is the traditional fief of the sugar lords since the time of the Portuguese colonisation. The exploitation, the repression, the hunger, is tougher there than in the north.

It is there, in the most southern part of the *zona da mata*, that, during a discussion in the union of agricultural workers, they gave me the most precise description of the exodus of the cane cutters towards the slums, and the crumbling of rural labour into unequal groups, after the installation of the military dictatorship.

CLANDESTINOS AND
FICHADOS

The union headquarters is brand new. "We had
to increase the membership fee to fifty cruzeiros a month to pay for the construction,"
said the secretary of the union as we entered
the still unused place. The room looked like
a refectory. There was a table covered with
a waxed tablecloth, with a fruit and vegetable
motif in vivid colours. There was a black
table. A young woman is sitting in the back,
listening. The secretary is Black. Another
Black man, with a straw hat, sits down close
to him. Everyone pays attention. A studious,
meticulous poverty.

I asked how the living conditions of
the workers had evolved since 1964.

—From 1964 to 1968 things worked out,
more or less, said the secretary. From 1968
and onwards things have deteriorated wholly,
so much that it is hard to tell. They have
reduced the salaries. The salary is not augmen-
ted but once a year, and yet not in proportion
to the cost of living. The price of living essen-
tials, on the other hand, rises every day. And in
addition to that, the bosses always take a part

of the salary. So, the peasants quit the farms and move to the city.

(The ways of explaining these departures are different: the restraints on wages imposed by the patrons; the obligation of the workers to cut cane seven days a week; the system of *barracão*, that forces them to buy from the cantine, where everything is expensive; the absence of schools and hospitals in the countryside; the appropriation of *roças* by the bosses. Some people simply say: "I don't want to be a prisoner anymore." No matter which explanation one advances, the process is immense: people leave the country to live in the city.)

The secretary speaks about the oppressive atmosphere that the landlords impose on their farms.

—The worker who lives on the farm is constantly watched over by the manager. Often, the employers, the administrators, threaten the workers. Some resist, others leave. For my part, personally, they came to arrest me while I was working. A police investigator sent by the owners of the land. I resisted, and finally, I stayed. But more often, the peasants leave.

—And then?

—Then, when they have made it to the city, they come back and start to work as *clandestino*. That means that they work day by day, without a contract. Most of the *clandestinos* live in the slums—but not all; sometimes there are *clanestinos* on the plantations. Some of them work temporarily through the *empreiteros* system, recruiters that receive a percentage related to the workers they manage to gather for the patrons. The others, those who have a contract, are called *fichados*, the "registered." They also say *direitos*, legals.

The number of *fichados* constantly decreases. The plantation patrons don't have any interest in contracts, because contracts mean that they have to pay the I. N. P. S. (social assurance funds) and other expenses. The *fichados* must be members of the union and the membership fee is automatically deducted from their wages.

(In the past decades, the number of workers in France "without status," inter-mediary, subcontracted, etc. has been rapidly increasing. Cleavages within the workforce and the multiplication of precarious groups. I am always surprised to discover the unity of capitalist administration, the richest centres relying on the most miserable. How does the system penetrate this far with such precision?)

—In our *municipio*, continues the secretary, the majority of workers are *clandestinos*. The truck picks up half of them in the slums of the *municipio*, the other half outside. After 1968 the migration from the farms to the cities accelerated.

—Since the appropriation of the *roças*?

(The global price of sugar boomed, the patrons wanted to plant sugarcane everywhere. The repression was harder than ever in the countryside: who could stop them?)

—Yes. Here we call them *sitios*, kitchen gardens.

—And how is it going?

—Among 8000 agricultural workers in the *municipio*, about 2500 are *fichados*, and the rest *clandestinos*. Some temporary workers come from afar, from the *agreste*, to work fifteen days on the plantations. They are called *corumbas*. The period of cane crushing corresponds to an important movement for all *clandestinos*, *corumbas*, *boias frias*: the trucks carry whole loads, picked up by recruiters in the cities, shanty towns, villages.

We speak about payment. The *fichados*, explains the secretary, have a notebook where the count is written. Recently the minimum wage was 37.04 cruzeiros a day. That's what they note on the "slip." But if the workers exceed the norm, they get another payment, non-declared, in another notebook, and for that they make a complementary sheet each fifteen days.

The workers around the table intervene: the explanation by the secretary doesn't seem totally accurate. Everyone gives their own version. The secretary answers by picking it up again and ends up completely lost in this little arithmetic of misery. The astuteness of the accountancy that we don't manage to disentangle concerns one or two francs a day, sometimes centimes. There is, in the contrast between this meticulousness of status, files, retentions, calculations, differences (a detailed organisation of fractions of the workforce) and the derisory sums paid out, something crushing.

A man comes in. Tall, slender, open shirt, glasses. An active air. It is the lawyer of the union (and the other unions of the state). Could he explain it to us? He draws columns on the black board: the *clandestinos*, like the *fichados*, receive an official slip every day with the minimum wage, one slip every week, one slip every fifteen days... He writes down the numbers. It doesn't tally. It becomes confusing once more.

Leave the details of the payslip, says the lawyer. What's essential is to understand the mechanism of readjustment of the annual salary, which is supposed to catch up with inflation, and that each time gnaws on the salaries of the workers. The wage rise, that the government undertakes each year in the month of May, only concerns the minimum wage. Thus, the salary was raised, by decree, from 37.04 to 54.80 in May of last year. But since the workers now earn between sixty and eighty cruzeiros, by piece, the readjustment doesn't give them anything. So, the government can announce they have raised the salaries by 44.6% even though the workers wouldn't notice any difference, and, on the contrary, are more impoverished each day, insofar as the prices are rising.

The lawyer then speaks about the development of the conditions of the agricultural workers since 1964. He works, for many years, in different *municípios* in the state. He has managed to collect figures, and is far-sighted. He distinguishes stages in the repression and the exodus (the two are related).

—In 1964 the government implemented the "intervention" (the authoritarian replacement of leadership) in thirty-two rural unions in the State of Pernambuco.

In 1968 and1969 the patrons thought they had won the "revolution." They began mass expulsions. This was the terrible period of the president Médici. In 1972 the entire world was frightened. The minister of work had suppressed the immunity of the delegates. With Geisel, things started to become better. But at this moment, 70% of workers had already been thrown out on the street. We are heading towards 80%. As there have been fewer "interventions" in the northern zone of the state, there have been fewer expulsions. But the south, where we are, was a region where many peasant

leagues settled, and experienced terrible
repression after 1964.

From 1974 to 1978 we faced a transitional
period. The government "interventions" in
the unions halted. It again became a question
of applying the laws of work. For us the situation was ambiguous. We could freely address
our complaints to the authorities as long as
we didn't say anything to the press. As soon
as we made something public, the repression
beat down on us. The police even kept an eye
on the internal bulletins of the unions and we
couldn't express ourselves openly.

—And now, do you think that a new period
is starting?

—Listen, soon a general strike in cane must
break out, if the patrons don't accept a salary
increase of 100%, the return of the *tabelas*
(a general norm of yield) and other rights that
we demand. With the outbreak of this strike, we
will see whether we are in a new period or not.

(We will clearly see if the police enter
the unions, if the persons in charge will be
locked up and beaten, if the armed guards
of the latifundia open fire on the strike
picket... Everyone around the table thought
about what the lawyer said, who had now
fallen silent.)

A moment of waiting.

The rasping voice of an old and toothless
Black man breaks the silence:

—Here, hunger is the problem. I often sleep
without eating. I earn fifty-two cruzeiros
a day (about 7.50 francs). My wife keeps asking
me what I am going to do to feed my eight
children. Sometimes we don't have more than
a little fish for them to share.

He raises his head and looks at us one
by one and says with a doleful tone—the rasping
voice becoming a real moaning:

—I am hungry like a mare in a rut! People
here are suffering too much. How could ten
people live on fifty cruzeiros a day?

(Yes, how could seventy cents a day
be enough for each person? Try to think
for a moment...

—But that is something else, over there
everything is much cheaper...

—No, only the people themselves don't cost
anything. The meat costs, in the villages of the
North-East of Brazil, almost as much as here.
To eat at a restaurant you pay as much as you
do in Paris. In Recife, on the beach, a glass of
coconut water, fresh from the coconuts that
you see everywhere, costs about ten cruzeiros,
1.50 francs.

—The fruit harvest, the products of
the countryside?

—Almost nothing. The sugar has eaten
everything. You only find food in the stores.)

It is sunset. The windows become tinged
with a red that spreads around the table.

The old man repeats that he is hungry.
His face is wrinkled, one imagines bloodstained
reflections.

—You live at the farm?
—Yes, for twenty-five years.
—Are you a *fichado*?
—Yes, yes, I have all the documents
in the world!

To die of hunger with all the documents in
the world; contract of employment, assurances,
payslips. To die of hunger for the "exportation
model" and income receipts.

The more I gathered witnesses and information, the more the hunger appeared to
me, with terrible clarity, as both material and
product of a refined complicated dispositive.
The hunger was not a simple, spectacular
absence, almost accidental, of disposable food—
as they present it to us, when they want us to
believe that charity, and "first aid," would be
enough to stop it. The hunger of the North-
East was an essential part of what the military
power called the "development" of Brazil.
It was not a simple hunger, a primitive hunger.
It was an elaborate hunger, an advanced
hunger, a hunger to be booming, in one word,
a modern hunger. I saw it rise in waves, called
economic plans, development projects, industrial centres, incentive measures of investment,
mechanisation and modernisation of agriculture.
Much work was needed for this hunger. In
fact, a large number of people worked flat out

for it. One dealt with it in buildings, bureaus, palaces and all sorts of posts of command and control. This hunger buzzed of buying orders on telex, credit lines in dollars, marks, yen, feverish operations on the *commodities markets* (the stocks of raw material, where the speculators sell, resell, buy, buy again, ten, fifteen or thirty times the same batch of sugar, of cacao or cotton before it has even been harvested, making the rate fal or grow, always in order to beat and dispossess the direct producer), of land transactions, anticipations, tricks and good deals. The details of the production of this hunger were abyssal. Shopkeepers, bankers, shipowners, company managers, experts, businessmen all had their part, and an army of middlemen, brokers and merchants too. And bureaus of studies, planning institutes. And army generals, politicians, policemen, and entire administrations. And all these people managed to make commissions, benefits, profits, rents, interest rates and advantages out of this hunger... Yes, really, the meticulous organisation of the development of this hunger appeared to me as something prodigious.

This hunger, through its own characteristics, merged with the development of the mode of production. A monoculture of sugar, a monotony of food. A slow-acting, patient hunger, a nibbling hunger, a hunger growing to the rhythm of the market economy. The systematic production of subaltern humanity, reduced to an almost vegetative existence, but one from which capitalism draws a workforce.

Is it not a miracle, that the modern political economy, manages, by the force of patience (every penny counts: they scrape off the hourly salary here, to fiddle the inflation index there, elsewhere recovering twenty square metres of kitchen garden to plant sugar-cane), to transform everything into hunger: the labour, the harvest, the subventions, the investments?

Everyone was incorporated in this economy of hunger by their own adequate means: from the experts and desk-workers to the nomads, from the permanent to the temporary, the workers, the small-scale owners... I discovered, while doing the inquiry among agricultural workers and small farmers of the *zona da mata*, the complexity of the crushing system that took them on in the soil of *agreste*, in the sugar plantations, in the shanty towns and the crossroads where the trucks picked up the workers, and dragged them away from their crops and parcels, that depreciated their harvests and their work, that divided them into multiple categories, that expelled them into other regions.

This old starving worker was supplied with "all the documents in the world."

That small producer was ruined by a too great harvest.

SMALL-SCALE
PROPERTY OWNERS

At the border between the *zona da mata* and the *agreste*, in the east of the state of Pernambuco, small-scale property owners are involved in the meetings of the agricultural workers. The frontier is not rigid between the real landowner, provided with a title, but without more than a few hectares of sparse soil, the *posseiro*, possessor of soil without title, always threatened by expulsion, the sharecropper, the contract worker, the dayworker, the permanent worker who conserves a little parcel of earth. Yes, theoretically, before 1964, when there was a certain freedom of organisation, the peasant league regrouped the small-scale property owners to fight for the right to the earth and the agricultural workers' union for the raising of wages, the two often overlapped. And the league has always claimed the same base for recruitment as the union, and has been searching, when it was possible, to ally itself with it. Even today, after fifteen years of repression, dismantling, torture, the executions, I find traces of this entanglement.

A *município* in the east of the state.
The union counts small-scale owners among
its members. About thirty out of a hundred
of their members are small-scale owners or
posseiros. The president of the union himself,
installed "by intervention" by the dictatorship
in 1964, owns six hectares.

A little group of peasants. Black, *caboclos*,
one or two of them are white. Small surfaces.

—I am a *posseiro*, says a Black man, I have
four hectares.

—I have two.

—Can you live on two hectares?

—No, you can do nothing. (He grimaces.)
It is dry soil, without irrigation. I also work as
a mason, aside from that, to be able to live.

An old peasant announces he owns ten
hectares. Cassava, fruits. "*Tenho leitura,*" he adds
to the inventory of his possessions: I can read.

—The agricultural workers want their salaries to increase. And the small-scale owners
that are here, what do they want?

It is the old man who "has reading" that
answers. The others approve what he says by
nodding their heads.

—To be finished with the bureaucracy of
the banks and the power, to get loans of money
with low interest rates, to equip ourselves.
To create cooperatives to guarantee the price
of the products. For the moment, all over
the state of Pernambuco, there are only a dozen

collectives, which is nothing. This question
of price is vital for small-scale owners. For the
moment, we are crippled. Take for example
the price of *feijão* in the *agreste* last year. When
we planted them we paid 1200 for each sack
of *feijão*. Everyone went into debt to be able
to pay for the seeds. And when we sold them,
after the harvest, that was great, we got three
hundred cruzeiros for each sack! Many sold
their entire harvest without being able to pay
back the banks. A good harvest thus forces
us into even more misery! Everywhere it's the
same. In the *mata*, in the *agreste*. What we
harvest doesn't have any value. The greater
the harvest, the greater the hunger.
  —Still, food is sold very expensively.
Where is the difference going?
  —The trade. Here reigns the trade of
the devil. There is no control. The harvest
lasts three months, it is a crazy period.
The traders want to buy everything at a low
price. Afterwards, they sell it expensively.
The government doesn't intervene. In reality,
the government doesn't care about anything
other than exportation.

THE EXPORTATION

We are familiar with the general mechanism that cripples the populations of the Third World; it has often been analysed. The export-driven economy. The agriculture of these countries doesn't serve to feed their populations, but to obtain a trade surplus. With the exception of the consumption in some small industrialised pockets where most of the disposable goods go, the rest—that is destined for the interior markets, to satisfy local needs—is considered a loss. The combined pressure from the creditor states, the International Monetary Fund, the holding firms of advanced technology, the banks, the military-political centres, forces the countries that are dependent upon them to turn an ever greater part of their economy towards export, to search with frenzy for the keys to growth in the importation of capital and technology, in the influx of investments. That which is called "development."

But this form of the economy goes together with an ever-growing debt. Loans and their interest must be paid. The debt becomes

a cancer that wears down the cells of the local
economy one by one. The spiral brings about
more and more exports. Groundnuts, cotton,
coffee, sugar, cacao, rice, wood, meat. Everywhere, in the Third World, subsistence crops
destined for the populations fall. Our stores
are full of sugar, oil, chocolate, meat, and our
heavy industries with the raw materials they
devour. Over there, the peasant loses his earth,
the rural exodus inflates the slums. The food
deficiencies are rising and, sometimes, in
a leap, starvation engulfs hundreds of millions
of men, women and children.

The more the economies of the Third
World open up to the global markets, the
more the mass of the population falls into
destitution—while some few locals take off
and the power of multinational companies
grows each year.

The military regime that was installed
in 1964 emphasised the opening of Brazil
to foreign capital. Fifteen years later, in 1979,
the country's foreign debt reached the
prodigious sum of fifty billion dollars. One
of the largest foreign debts in the world.
The sum appears abstract. But it has an
immediate concrete significance: each year
the country has to pay seven billion dollars
in interest, independent of the pay-off. The
running debt alone requires more and more
sugar, coffee, minerals to be sold... The debt

is a pump that syphons off resources to richer countries.

And within Brazil, the Central-Southern region (Rio de Janeiro-São Paulo), and some other well-defined islands within this immense territory, concentrate all the disposable resources for industrial development, and there accumulates the money, the equipment, the technique, the cadre, the means of research, and thus reproduces the same relationship of exploitation and pillage towards the distant North-East and other subaltern regions, as the big imperialist powers maintain with the entire country of Brazil.

The North-East, with its thirty-five million inhabitants, is a country apart. Some say a colony. A camp, wrote Francisco Julião, leader of the peasant league exiled after the *coup d'État*:

"No one that has seen and studied the North-East has been able to hold back a cry of revolt in front of this concentration camp where twenty million starving human creatures are suffering. The peasants of the North-East, anxious about the earth, monitored by the big landowners, flagellated by the drought, are all Brazilians, those who travel the most and settle the least. We meet them everywhere, courageous, enterprising, and obsessed with their country, with the earth that is associated with freedom, water, abundance, the horses.

The departure is useless, the flight in vain. It is the same thing everywhere: the plantations of hevea in the Amazon, of rice in São Francisco, of coffee in Parana." [*Cambão – The Yoke: The Hidden Face of Brazil*]

The political economy of the military regime has accelerated the uprooting of the population. The freedom given to the land-lords to evict the sharecroppers and the owners of small parcels, the extension of the sugar and exportation cultures, the massive sale of land to multinational companies (Péchiney, Volkswagen and many others have used their profits in Brazil to acquire immense areas), the systematic elimination of *posseiros* (possessors of land who don't carry a title), land speculation, the politics of grand projects and development centres, have multiplied the bleeding points.

In the industrial South they call these immigrants from the interior, hunted by the North-East misery, *pau de arara* (named after the sparsely equipped truck in which they are grouped for the trip). The construction sites of the "miracle" have drained them to the working class suburbs of the Centre-South, in the iron mines of Minas, or engulfed them in the Transamazon open to the forest and almost immediately after closed again by the rain and the mud. The film *Iracema*, whose main character is a young indigenous

prostitute jolting around in a truck between
groups, in huts and improvised brothels, shows
one of these cargo loads of workers that
a human trafficker negotiates in domain after
domain in the Amazon, as they once did with
the slaves: men and women for sale for all
kinds of work, with some prostitutes as a bonus,
thousands of kilometres away from where they
come from.

Some will simply die at the foot of the skyscrapers in Rio de Janeiro, or against the fences
of the subway under construction, small piles
of humans huddled up under rags, too weak
or too weary to keep on begging. The stressed
passersby won't notice them any longer.

I remember being cold between these
skyscrapers on the avenue Rio Branco, the
great artery of commerce, when, in the middle
of December 1976, during the tropical winter,
I went from one bureau to another looking
for data on the Brazilian economy. It was more
than thirty degrees, and this warmth in
December failed to warm me.

AN ECONOMIST

In Rio de Janeiro, in 1976, I met Maria da Conceição Tavares, one of the most well-known economists in the foundation of the ECLAC [UN's Economic Commission for Latin America and the Caribbean], who has been playing a key role in the formation of the doctrines of development on the continent. I asked her an entire series of questions on the economic situation. And, finally, this one:

—In your opinion, what will happen?

She had, up until then, been giving long answers, snapping back quickly, on every point I raised. Her reply was extensive, full of figures, on inflation, the Brazilian cycle in its relationship to the global capitalist cycles, the share of equipment in imports, the foreign debt, the disproportion between industries in the matrix of exchange—speaking fast, with the kind of furious dryness common to many of the Portuguese intellectuals, retained throughout many years far from Portugal.

She later interrupted herself, as if she was surprised by my question. She stared at me and said:

—What will happen? Well, nothing!
Nothing will happen. It will continue to stagnate like that...

And the obviousness of the immense rotting that all these figures designated seized me.

III
THE AWAKENING
OF A PEASANTS MOVEMENT

This Sunday, September 30th, will remain
an important date for the sugarcane workers
of Pernambuco. The unions of twenty-two
municipios have organised general assemblies
where they will vote on a strike. One hundred
thousand workers are concerned. Some days
ago two *municipios*, in São Lourenço da Mata
and Pau d'Alho, already voted for the strike:
on Monday, October 1st, when the legal dead-
line expires, the 18 000 workers of this zone
will cease to work. This entire procedure—a
secret vote in general assemblies summoned
by the official unions, the opening of negotiations with patrons and the Ministry of Labour
during the period when it is forbidden to strike,
a notice before the beginning of the movement—is prescribed by the infamous "strike
law" introduced by the dictatorship. Only
if this law is rigorously respected, will the strike
be considered "legal" (and they suppose,
but without certitude, that this will prevent
the people in charge of the union from being
thrown in prison at the beginning of the
movement).

A legal strike in the State of Pernambuco
would constitute a beginning: in none of the
social conflicts that have burst out in Brazil
these last years has it been possible to bring
together all the conditions required by the
"strike law." Until now. And, in the eyes of
a large number of workers, this "strike law"
is essentially a law that forbids strikes, tied
up by procedures of "conciliation," that the
authoritarian regimes know how to cook up.
However, things don't seem so predetermined
this end of September in the sugar regions.
Couldn't it be in the interest of a government,
engaged in an facelift operation called "opening,"
to let at least one legal strike take place – to
show that all strikes aren't forbidden and
defend a law attacked from all directions?

See how complicated the situation is:
some people say that the sugar patrons themselves wouldn't be hostile to a strike movement
that would allow them to call for the government to raise the price of sugar (which is bought
by the National Institute of Sugar at a fixed
price). One must, without a doubt, consider
this rumour with caution: I have seen, here
and there, plantation and factory owners sup-
pressing "strike agitation" with vigour and
threatening workers with reprisals at the sight
of the slightest movement. On their side, the
unions gathered in the FETAP [the Federation
of Agricultural Workers of Pernambuco] count

on the preparation for this strike to strengthen
their position and react to a situation ever
more catastrophic. But could they really engage
in a direct confrontation with the sugar patrons?

Anyhow, the workers are ready to do
something. So it is – the hunger, the misery, has
reached such a level, that to relinquish means
to die in silence. An immediate wage increase is
necessary.

Uncertainties, rumours, fears, hopes.
They mobilise in the countryside of the state,
for the vote on September 30th. Principally,
the peasant assemblies are held behind closed
doors, without journalists. They fear police
raids, and certain electoral procedures might
be sensitive, given the complexity of the
disposition of the strike law and the workers'
differing statuses (and the vagueness in the
interpretation of the number of unionised
workers and the quorum). The unionised
prefer the lowest possible number of external
observers. But Antonio, a friend and "assistant" in the union (as the collaborating economists, accountants and lawyers are called –
often members of Church organisations such
as 'Pastoral da Terra,' which isn't the case with
Antonio), will take me to the assembly, on
the condition that I carry a correct and valid
accreditation, for if there is any trouble.

We leave on Saturday, because Antonio
needs to participate in a preparatory meeting

for the assembly, and a final distribution
of pamphlets on the plantations.

On the bus that takes us to the city
N., Antonio tells me how the directory board
of the union, including the "assistants," had
been summoned in Recife some days ago:
"They told us that the place belonged to the
Labour Inspection. But when we came there,
we were confronted by the National Information Service (the secret police). A colonel,
about sixty years old, very courteous, gave
us a lecture in economics: Why do you go on
strike? The patrons can't pay. Do you know
the price of sugar? Do you know that there is
a crisis? Miguel, the president of the union,
responded that the patrons are always com-
plaining, but everything works out fine for
them—as the recent doubling of the area cultivated with sugar proves. The colonel, himself
from a family of sugar patrons, was polite and
pleasant with us, but when we were leaving,
we were supervised by two sinister-looking
guys that sent a shiver down my spine."

We have now reached N., a big market
town. It's a scramble when the bus arrives.
We go directly to the seat of the union.

We go up to the second floor of a little blue-coloured building, whose first floor is reserved for the medical activities of the union: dentist, pharmacy... In the stairs and corridors, agricultural workers, wearing the straw hats of cane cutters, go back and forth. Women and children are crowded into a kitchen corner. The meeting room is quite big. Wooden chairs are stacked up in a row in the far end of the room, as in a cinema. The walls are pink with some posters. The window overlooks a wide expanse, a square and an empty plot.

Antonio introduces me. A very fat man, soaked in sweat, who looks like a Mexican character in a movie (one of those enormous innkeepers that embodies, in the old black and white movies, the despair, alcoholism, the wretched traffic of a mythical Latin America at the end of the world) rushes at me and repeats a phrase that I don't manage to capture until the third repetition: "What is your name?" pronounced in approximate French. He speaks loudly. Do I know Brazil? Do I know 'Pitu' (a brand of sugarcane alcohol)? He takes me to the kitchen to make me a drink, a glass of Pitu. With his badly shaved face, his bulging eyes, his checked grey shirt open to the waist, I think he has a likeable and vulnerable air. They remind him: the meeting will begin. No Pitu. He resigns to the table in front of an antique typewriter and starts to type with two fingers—he functions as a secretary at the union.

They speak about the propaganda in the plantations for tomorrow's assembly. A Black man speaks about threats that he has received from the *dono de engenho* (the patron of the plantation). The *cabo* (foreman) of the plantation became mad at him because he invited peasants to the assembly.

—I said to the *cabo*: I am the father of a family, like you: I'm not looking for trouble. He answered me: you agitate the people, you are an agitator and a striker. I said to him: I am the person in charge of the union at the plantation. What happens happens.

—You know our movement is legal, says Antonio. This very day we will visit a plantation where they forbade us from distributing pamphlets a couple of days ago, and this time we will do it under police protection, because the judge gave us the right.

The Black man nodded in agreement, moderately convinced.

Everyone describes the conditions in the plantations that they know. They try

to predict how many workers will come to
the assembly.

—In Serra?

—They are frightened. They are
clandestinos. Seven hundred people work there,
in cutting and clearing at the mill.

—Are they all afraid?

—Most of them. About twenty might show
up to the assembly.

They also speak about a nearby shanty
town, whose inhabitants they hope they can
convince to come.

—Don't worry, says Antonio, the world
wasn't built in a day. The important thing is
that people understand why there is a strike.
If they want to take part, they take part. (He
turns to me and adds:) These fifteen years have
left marks: everyone is frightened. (Again, to
the meeting:) If they don't come, the work will
continue next week. If they are frightened and if
they don't come to the assembly tomorrow, then
we have to go see those who haven't shown up
and ask them why they are afraid.

They gather around the table to give
details about this or that plantation. There are
dozens of people. In the middle of them, Miguel,
the president of the union, is seated—brown,
a large face, a big moustache; he is not an agricultural worker, but a small-scale property
owner; trained by the Church. He was installed
during the "intervention," after the putsch

in 1964. The "Mexican" types noisily on his writer. They try to set the agenda for the day. Everybody speaks at the same time. Hubbub. High-pitched laughter from the Mexican. At the end of the table, two men, gaunt, with wizened faces, wearing black hats, remain silent and impassive. These two men, they told me, were among the founders of the peasant league in N., in the beginning of the 1960s. They are now members of the union, but something in their attitude keeps them apart.

A tall and slim young man, João, holds in his hand a list of the people who must take part in the meeting and calls them. João, "assistant" of the union, is employed by the 'Pastoral da Terra,' one of the organisations of the Church in rural areas. Everyone raises their hand when their name is called. It calms down. The Mexican moves his typewriter to another table. The reunion will really begin.

I look at the posters and inscriptions around me. They are advertisements for ploughing equipment, fertilisers, pesticides, on which they have added pencilled slogans: "The union gives strength." "Everything depends on each person's efforts." "Work builds Brazil." One sign runs with big stencilled letters: "The authority that restricts or tries to restrict the legitimate exercise of the strike will be taken to court in accordance with the current legislation. Article 31 of the strike law."

—The meeting can't take more than an hour, announces Antonio. Then, he tells me, we have to transport a sick man. We have to provide the car, always the union assistance. We are overwhelmed by these medical tasks.

Antonio explains to everyone how the voting will unfold tomorrow. Each one of the inscribed will receive an envelope with two ballot papers: "*sim*," of green colour, in favour of the strike, "*não*," of yellow colour, against.

—Does one have to say something when one votes?, asks the Mexican at the other end of the table.

—No, answers Antonio, you put the vote in the ballot box without saying anything. And when someone has voted, they have to sign or put their fingerprint on the voting list.

A scene interrupts this explanation that everyone is carefully listening to. Miguel, the president, sharply questions a redhead with a moustache, orange shirt and a hat, who stands back and is also listening. "Are you a member of the union?" – "Yes." – "Your card!" He puts it up. Miguel looks at it, suspicious. "Okay, that's good, have a seat." The man laughs: "I prefer to stand."

Antonio starts again: "We need to hurry with the voting procedure because we might have as many as three thousand people. If we drag on, it might take ten hours. We need to

finish in five or six hours. We divide the voters
into six sections."

—What is the quorum? somebody asks.

—One thousand two hundred, answers
João.—And who has the right to vote? Only
the members of the union?—Yes, one has
to be enrolled on the lists.—Not really, says
another. A complicated discussion follows.

During this time they discover that the
man in an orange shirt is the cousin of one of
the people in charge of the union. They call to
him: "Come, come, comrade, we didn't know,
you should have told us, take a seat at the
table." They surround him, flock around, and
offer him a seat. The president: "Some years
ago a guy we didn't know came to a meeting,
then he walked to the Fourth Army and told them
that we were organising a subversive meeting.
You understand? Do you excuse me, comrade?"

Antonio tries to overcome the effusions
in order to proceed with João about the distribution of the six sectors between the people
in charge. Each one will be responsible for
about six hundred potential voters, grouped
according to a plantation. "Are there any
questions?"—"Yes, I have one. I haven't been
given any sector. What will I do?"—"You will
agitate in the hall."

They go through the necessary expenses:
pens, the straw mats they use to make polling
booths.

João: "We need snacks. Otherwise, people will leave before the vote has ended, this is what happened in S."

They count the money necessary to buy bread and fruit juice. The treasurer arrives, greying, middle-aged, he stays at the entrance. Miguel hails him. (Antonio explains to me: "He is a bit afraid and tries to stay out of this. Miguel wants to implicate him, therefore he wants him to buy bread for the assembly.") The union is poor, every cent counts. Finally, everything is decided. Around the table, they let out a sigh of relief.

As the meeting breaks up, my eyes fall on an article in an old yellowed journal on a desk cluttered with signs: "*Social life*. Antonia S. Teixeira, one of the most beautiful and most elegant figures of the society of Recife will tomorrow receive the greetings from her friends on the occasion of her birthday."

The cement floor is dirty red, the ceiling is crumbling.

—Let's go, says Antonio.

PAMPHLETS
IN THE SUGAR FIELDS

We leave the union. The square in front of
the place is very dirty. The smell of cattle
is hanging in the air. Of black goats. Of fruit
waste. The side path is full of puddles and
garbage. Parked trucks. Surprised by an
intense warmth, under this grey sky. This insis-
tent greyness, I don't manage to associate it
with the word "tropical." Something derisory.
A phrase from a painter friend from Recife
comes to mind: "I spent my childhood reading
French literature and dreaming about one day
going to one of these 'tropical countries' that
are described in the books. What a deception
when I realised that our North-East carries
exactly this name..."

So the big affair today is a distribution of
pamphlets for which the judge ordered police
protection, on a plantation where they ejected
union members by force some days before.

We are packed in a jeep, direction: the
police. Jolts on the trajectory. A little village,
a sloping street, coloured houses. The *delegacia
da policia*, a beige and blue building, with
a narrow veranda and an exterior staircase.

Two cops in front of the door. Miguel enters with another person in charge of the union. Waiting in the jeep. Antonio, nervous, moves back and forth. The others are silent. Grey sky, a little wind, and the heat that comes back as the wind stops blowing.

The village is silent. Mules pass, going along, one by one, the different coloured houses—ochre, light red, blue, beige. A yellow barrel—a stain. Far away, mountains block the horizon. Another of these spaces one feels could enclose oneself forever. The waiting here seems infinite.

Miguel finally leaves the police office. He holds his hat in his hand, there is something a bit stooping in his gait. A plain-clothed police-man goes with him, short haircut, sunglasses, he really looks the part. The cop says some words to him on the doorstep, patting his shoulder in a protective gesture, then dismisses him and goes back into the commissariat. Miguel comes back to us, the hat still in his hand, alone. "*Não vai dar?*" asks the worried union member in front of me in the car ("It wont work?"). Miguel says that the police have given instructions directly to the security service of the plantation. No need for an escort: they will let us distribute pamphlets.

We go again, in two cars. In the other is the Mexican with the megaphone of the union. A horrible earth trail is rising through the hills on the road to the 'Usina Nosso Senhor da Serra,' to which the soil belongs. Just before arriving, Miguel stops the jeep and assures himself that everything is in order. If anything happens, could he say that I am a journalist? – Yes. He nervously turns his leather cowboy hat in his hands. "We recapitulate. We are all members of the union. He (he points toward Antonio) is an assistant of the union, and he (he points toward me) is a reporter. We are going to distribute pamphlets and speak to people through loudspeakers. But we can't arrange any meetings. The police said: pamphlets are okay, but no meetings."

We are at a height. An immense view, wind. As a conjuration against the henchmen and latifundia armies, our jeep carries, on both of its sides, the inscription that I noted in the union space: "The authority that restricts or tries to restrict the legitimate exercise of the strike..."

Everyone's gathering around Miguel who tries out the loudspeakers. The sound hits the mountain and comes back. "*Uma beleza!*" A wonder!

We take off together. We enter the plantation territory and our megaphone begins to call for an assembly tomorrow.

A first, surreal image of this foray of the union on the soil of the sugar plantations: a megaphone shouting in empty fields.

Without a doubt they aren't, and there are people dispersed in the dense and green mass. But for the moment only silence answers us. Here is the factory. The smell of sickly, sweet molasses. A guardian, a gun in his belt, in front of the bureau. Miguel presents himself, the guardian takes him to the "major" in charge of the security of the factory. It is okay, the distribution can start. Our little convoy goes back in the same direction it came from.

They throw pamphlets on the road out through both of the cars. Again the uncanny silence of the cane. And then, appearances. First, a little group of women and children comes out of nowhere and carefully picks up the small squares of paper scattered on the ground. Then two men, who show up on the trail, take pamphlets and disappear. Then a group of workers with a foreman. They hesitate for a short while (due the presence of the foreman), and then pick up pamphlets.

Again, nobody is in sight, but all our pamphlets are removed from the trail, as if the sugar fields drank our propaganda in silence. The megaphone dies out, because we drive quite fast and the engine is maybe not as good as we thought. A Black man, who is sitting in front of me in the back of the jeep, is getting nervous: "One hears: *Trabalhor rural!* and nothing else." Oh, one would like a louder voice, to break the silence of the fields...

Here is a crossing of trails. A building (the *bodega* of the plantation) and two parked trucks, full of a dense crowd, maybe a hundred people. Always the same spectacle of the trucks with *boias frias*: rags, straw hats, tools, bags. But in Princess Serrana we saw them before work. Now, at five o'clock in the evening, I am struck by the dishevelled faces that the day has undone, particularly by the small exhausted faces of the children. Antonio has to think the same. He shouts in the megaphone: "We know that it is a sacrifice to go to the assembly on Sunday. But you have to, for your wages. Come! We will try to send a truck to pick you up. Even if only one of you comes!" A man, barefoot, jumps on the ground. In the truck, a very excited hubbub, everyone speaks at once. The union members arrange a meeting at a crossroads for tomorrow, and pass it on, shouting. A kid, shirt and ripped-up shorts, has taken a bundle of pamphlets and started to distribute them, carefully, one by one. Antonio repeats his discourse to the other truck. Extraordinary attention in these toothless faces, covered by beards, crushed by fatigue. And when we leave, Antonio shouts again: "It is legal! They don't have the right to stop the distribution of pamphlets! If anyone says the contrary, shut him up!"

Again the trail and the silence of the sugar-cane fields. The night falls, fresh, on the hills. The road, the headlights. Stopping again. We are at the foot of a *favela* [slum] whose houses spread over a slope, on both sides of a dirt road. We have barely parked our two jeeps when a police car shows up under our nose. The cops look at Antonio who is launching his call into the megaphone: "Attention, rural workers, there is an assembly tomorrow at eight o'clock! Come everyone, *clandestinos* and *fichados* alike!" He enumerates the demands. The Mexican and João start to distribute pamphlets. A group of children immediately gather around us, some of them carry other children in their arms. The police car takes off again.

Our little group sets out on a slow ascent on the weakly lit central street of the slum. Megaphone. Pamphlets. "Two days of work for one kilo of salty meat, is that reasonable, comrades?" An old Black woman, dressed in a headscarf, a pipe in her mouth, looks impassively at us, leaning on the window door to her shack which, like all *senzalas* (slave houses) looks like a stable box with an open top. An old man shouts: "I will come! I am a comrade of the union! I will come!" A meeting is improvised around a drunken man who shouts in misery, a bottle of booze in his hand.

Silhouettes of mountains indent the clear night. Around us, a few lights shine and one distinguishes the red-brown colour of the firmly packed earth that constitutes two sad straight streets. At this crossroad, a group of Black and mixed-race people, *caboclos*, crowd together to listen to Antonio: "We can't expect anything from the government, or the politicians. To wait means to die of hunger! What the union does is legal, it is no sub-version. You don't have to worry. The only thing you need to fear is hunger." People applaud, say: "Very good!" He continues: "We know that many are afraid to strike, but we propose it because we know that it's our sole means for change! I know that women, in particular, are afraid. I am addressing myself to them. The right to strike is in the constitution, it is legal." Miguel, the president of the union, speaks in his turn: "Your children don't have milk. You are criminals if you don't come to the meeting!" A little group is listening. Many children suffer from rickets, folded limbs, and swollen stomachs.

Our march through the streets of earth starts up again. "Tomorrow we will measure the fear," Antonio says. Mud, dirty water, naked children, a stinking heap of garbage. An abrupt descent among the houses carved out in the rocks.

The Mexican has found a "Pitu" bar and wants, by any means, to drag me there. He calls me the "Portuguese." He is blind drunk.

In the evening, after our return to N., Antonio tells me that he is afraid that this strike will fail, that there will be provocations. He has just finished reading *Germinal*, and the end made him depressed.

The assembly of the agricultural cane workers of the *municipio* of N. will be held in a large gymnasium of a religious school that the Sisters have provided for the union. The school, candy pink, looks like a piece of pastry. It is surrounded by coconut trees and the remaining shrubs of an abandoned park.

Seven o'clock in the morning. Everything is prepared in the empty hall. At the end of the room, six ballot boxes, carefully arranged on small tables. Some banners, lost in the immensity of the gymnasium: "Either the patrons give us what we want, or we stop working." "A yellow vote is a vote for the patrons." "Vote green, the colour of the workers." "Workers united will never be defeated."

The agricultural workers start to settle on the cement tiers in silence. Most of them are *caboclos*. Clean shirts, hats. They remain motionless, accustomed to waiting. There are few women.

A group enters the hall. They're guided by Teresinha, employed by the union, one head higher. Their small sizes surprise me, and I can still hear the words of Nelson Chaves about the starvation that produces generations of dwarfs. There is something huddled up, closed, in their appearance and their way of walking, as if they were freezing inside. This incessant presence of hunger, in its sly form, rather, of a rodent sickness, than a spectacular state of emaciation. A rapid observer – who knows nothing of alimentary monotony, brain damage since birth or the progression of dwarfism – might not notice anything. On the plane from Paris, a young lady from the high society of Rio told me: "Are you going to the North-East? Oh, you will see, things have been changing for the better. You almost don't see hunger anymore." Why should hunger always be visible? The hunger that stunts the children in the bellies of their mothers, that slowly kills millions of peasants without a spectacle, isn't this hunger terribly efficient?

João, the other assistant, also leads a group. He is tall and looks like a giant among them. He explains to them that they must vote green, and that the yellow ballot paper means that one supports the patron. Gathered around João, they seem to belong to another species: reduced, shrivelled up, puny.

During this assembly I never stop reading the work of hunger in their faces and bodies, gestures and expressions.

Eight o'clock. An old, almost blind, Black woman, all dressed in white, gropes her way along.

A little group is formed around one of
the people in charge of the union, he of whom
they said yesterday: "You will be an agitator,"
and who today plays this role to perfection:
"We have to fight for the future of Brazil, for
our children. I have a full stomach, but we have
to think about others, and the future." He is
an old man, vivid, slim, with a grey moustache.
"We are all equals in front of the law, but you
are more slaves than during the times of slavery."

The gymnasium fills up gently. The public
address system deafens us with religious songs,
full of hallelujahs. The violent light of day is
filtered through a wire netting that covers the
triangular opening at the top of the cement
wall. Behind, one glimpses the palm tree tops
and an unusually blue sky.

More and more women and children
arrive. This thin crowd, in their Sunday best,
pour in silently (I think of a congregation of
Black believers, in a church in the US South),
it is early steps of the workers' movement,
in fear and hunger. Defeated, massacred, pur-
sued, it starts again here, indefinitely recreated
like the sea—always, just as the primitive
expropriation from where capital draws its
bloodstained substance, the enclosure of
the parcels, the exodus to the cities, the day
labourer's miserable wandering...

The little old man, elevated to "agitator,"
systematically continues with his speeches

among the tiers and moves around among the rows. There is, in his joyful and wrinkled eyes, something radiant.

The crowd becomes dense on the tiers. The agricultural workers, whose brown and Black faces are outlined against the shirts of bright, vivid colours, are very precisely aligned on the four ascending rows like small, clear and symmetrical figurines of lead.

A Black woman, at the entrance, is worried: "They told me that only those who *tem leitura* ("have reading," can read and write) are allowed in." Antonio reassures her and she enters. Again this impression of seeing a giant leading a group of Lilliputians. Antonio is robust, a bit red-tinted. Well-fed, like me. Suddenly I get the vision of our bodies stuffed with proteins, vitamins, vegetables, fruits, meat, the blood rushing in our vessels, our neurons completely fed, our entire machinery irrigated... And their bodies, poor bodies of flour and beans, weak limbs, slowly atrophied brains. Two species that savage capitalism dissociates in the midst of humankind. Whereas, following Gilberto Freyre, a very famous sociologist acclaimed by the official milieus here, the dominant culture tries to promote an image of Brazil as having achieved a harmonious fusion between the races and people in a novel unity, it is rather, on the contrary, a terrible break-up that strikes me here in Brazil, a break-up between white

and Black people, rich and poor, the well-fed
and starving, the educated and the illiterate.
Certain forms of segregation are reminiscent
of South Africa. And the truth of Brazil seems
much better summarised in these two verses
from the poet Carlos Drummond de Andrade,
than in the entire mythology of Freyre: "There
is no Brazil. But do, by chance, Brazilians exist?"

Miguel, the president of the union, starts
his first speech, noisily amplified by the public
address system. Others speak in turn. The
crowd applauds quietly after each intervention.

Antonio counts and recounts the audience, worried about the quorum. Miguel crosses
the hall in every direction, with his cowboy
hat, with the case of an attaché in his right hand
and a bottle of milk in the left. (While I'm
taking notes, a man passes in front of me, looks
at me as I am writing and looks up: close to
me, an inquiring, thin little face.)

Around half past ten, one of the members
says to Antonio: "The people are hungry, let's
begin." They begin.

Queues are formed for the vote, in front
of the six ballot boxes. They call up names.
People rush, bump into each other to get
in line.

Now starts the bizarre procedure of the
"legal strike": to queue for a strike like one is
queueing for a job. The hours of the voting are
absurd: only workers who want to strike have

come and a short vote by raised hands would
have been sufficient. One could profit from
this exceptional meeting with workers from
almost all plantations to start the practical
organisation of the movement. But the "strike
law" is conceived to exhaust everyone through
never-ending administrative procedures, and
it is in this way the voting unfolds, because the
union wants to respect the legal procedure.

In voting booth number two, the Mexican
runs around with his lists, envelopes, ballot
papers. The first voter comes, or, rather, is
thrown forward by the crowd. He takes out
his union card, unrolls an entire wallet where
the family photos are aligned under a trans-
parent plastic. It's an old man that slowly and
slantingly writes his signature down, while
the crowd behind him moves in order to decide
who's next. They show him the straw mat
curled up against the wall that functions as
a ballot booth. The second voter, does he know
how to write? No. A fingerprint on the list: the
Mexican makes him push a well-inked thumb
to the paper. The first comes back and puts his
envelope in the ballot box. A mess of papers.
The infernal heat of the crowd. During all
these procedures, for just two people, the crowd
is loosening itself and the Mexican starts
to shout: "Get in the line! Get in the line!"
(Go on strike "in a line"... How could you not
empathise with all those who, all over the

country, demand the abrogation of this "strike law" and a real right to strike in its place?)

Close to me, an old man, thin, grey-haired, white shirt, wrinkled tramp-style trousers, passes with an identity card in his hands which, I notice, is superimposed with the stamp **ANALFABETO** in big, blue letters. On his thumb the blue blot of the fingerprint. The sign of the illiterate. When leaving, he says to me, as if wanting to excuse himself: "I can sign, but it takes a long time, my hands shake too much." It is true, I've noticed that many hands shake when they write or even when they merely hold an object. The hunger.

Children want to vote. "How old are you?," asks Miguel, the president. They are fourteen or fifteen years old. "Too young. You need to be eighteen, it's the law," he tells them. "But your presence is important." The kids are disappointed. I ask them if they want to go on strike. They nod their heads, yes, they want to. These are the children that the law dismisses, deprived of schools, threatened by infirmity, they are the first to distribute pamphlets, propagate news, to run from one point to another in sight of the slightest movement. Small proletarians aged ten, twelve, fourteen years.

It is half past eleven. I leave the tumultuous voting lines to get some fresh air in town. My footsteps lead me to the only big and beautiful building in N., and I understand

why the poor are attracted to it. You live
in the midst of all this suffering, you walk
across the streets in search of respite and you
naturally find yourself in front of the church
that dominates the houses, and whose fresh
stillness provides you with shelter. You enter.
A *padre* officiates, magnificent in white and
golden clothes. Here is just auspiciousness,
softness, contemplation. The organ music pene-
trates you. Yes, it is indeed here that you find
comfort...

I come back around half past twelve.
Still a crowd. At Joãos voting table the spark-
ling face of a youngster that he allows to vote
runs toward the polling booth with his envelope. The situation improves. João, Antonio
and the others dispatch the votes through
a maximised simplification of formalities. Only
the Mexican hangs on to the details of the
procedure and thus produces a bottleneck.

I see the hands of agricultural workers
trembling too much to put the envelope in
the box, they need to repeat it three times.
The hunger.

At two they close the vote. A guy from
the Ministry of Labour comes. Vote counting.
There will be a strike.

NEGOTIATIONS
AND AGREEMENT

The twenty-two assemblies of the State of
Pernambuco taking place on this very Sunday,
September 30th, all voted in favour of
a strike. But the general strike of the sugarcane
workers will not occur. Only the eighteen
thousand workers in the two *municipios* that
had voted before the others ceased to work
on October 1st. The necessary negotiations
between the unions and the patrons ended in
an agreement on October 10th, on the eve
of the day scheduled for the outbreak of the
general strike.

The union demanded a 100% rise in
wages. They received 52%. The right to two
hectares of individual plots for each worker
was granted, as well as compensation for work-
days that are cancelled due to accidents. The
pay rise can't be but a provisional relief, during
this period when the inflation reaches almost
100% each year. When it comes to the other
clauses, their application is in question: aren't
80% of the cane workers *clandestinos*?

In the neighbouring State of Alagoas,
160 workers on a plantation of União de

Palmares went on strike; since the outbreak, five leaders have been put in prison by the plantation security that belongs to a sugar factory. They won't be released until after the strike is over, a strike that won't lead anywhere.

What would have been the first big legal strike in the country, thus, came to a sudden end. One could discuss the real range of the concessions of the employers. But something has happened, that sounds like a note of foreboding. The strike of the two *municipios*, the affluence of the assemblies of September 30th, the mobilisation in the plantations, announces the awakening of a peasant movement in the sugar regions of the North-East.

During these days, when the strike was being prepared, I travelled across many *municipios*, going from one union meeting to the next. During one of these sessions, I had an encounter that left a strong impression. I was asking questions to peasants about their living conditions, when a man entered. As he intervened in the discussion everyone suddenly fell silent, in a sign of respect. When he stopped talking they told me: "In front of you is João Virginio da Silva, the founder of the peasant league of Galiléia." He was an old man, dressed in a dark costume, sunglasses. He leaned on a cane. His look, his physiognomy, made me think of one of these old leaders of the Algerian National Liberation Front, that one feels has overcome the wounds, mutilations, sicknesses, to hold out, straight and standing upright, and whose simplicity, and worn elegance, inspires respect. The serious and calm voice of João Virginio da Silva strikes through with natural authority. "I am very glad to meet you," I told him. "What do you think of the present situation in this region?" – "I will only answer you at my place," he tells me. I thus take off with him to the farm in Galiléia.

As we walked slowly towards the square where we would take a cab, he stopped me and asked: "Do you think that the world has reached a stable condition, or that contradictions will continue to develop?" Surprised, I stayed silent for a while and then answered: "The contradictions will develop." – "I think the same thing," he said to me. And continued his march.

We reached his house after an hour in the car on chaotic roads. A poor shack, in naked cement, housed the local coffee house, in the midst of eroded hills scattered with small farming lands (for once there wasn't just sugar, but also onions, beans, some chickens). He made me sit down and said to his wife: "Bring the book." She came back with a big, red-coloured hardback volume, a Brazilian version of the *Encyclopaedia Britannica*. He showed me a photo of Christ (Do you recognise him? – Yes), a photo of Lenin (Him too? – Yes), of Kennedy (The same question – the same answer), the article on France, the article on Australia... He concluded: "The entire world is in this book. Well, you also find the peasant leagues." Read. He points out the article:

"*Peasant leagues.* Name given to organisations that have emerged in Pernambuco since 1955. Having as an objective an agrarian reform in the interest of the poor peasantry, the leagues became a movement on a nation-wide scale. A simple society of mutual aid, it was first founded on the plantation of Galiléia, *Município de Vitória de Santo Antão,* by Zézé in Galiléia. ... Later the leagues decided to react with force against the repression by the latifundistas in the region. Famous is the episode in Galiléia during which a dozens of peasants forced the government to expropriate soil in their favour after first having occupied it.

In 1963 there were a hundred leagues all over the country, counting more than 500 000 members. Just the council of the State of Pernambuco coordinated twenty-seven leagues with 120 000 affiliated members."

He closed the book carefully. He told me while pounding his words: "You see, they are obliged to speak about us. We have entered History."

We all silently listened to him. There was a woman, a small peasant and a teenager. The room was quite dark and through the light square of the window one could distinguish the hills surrounding the house. Something in the scene and among the characters inspired a sort of contemplation. João Virginio took up again: "I will answer the question you asked me. And then, I will tell you how the league of Galiléia was born, the first peasant league in Brazil.

You ask me what I think about the situation. The *coup d'État* has brought about at least one positive thing. The Brazilian army has now got to know the latifundistas. In the past we told them which kind of men they were. But they didn't believe us. They took power on the account of the latifundistas, but none of them had the political intelligence to help their so-called revolution. The destructive politics of these people finished by putting the president of the Republic in difficulty." (He spoke slowly, with a husky voice, but chose his words with such precision that one has the impression that he is pronouncing a written discourse.) "This is why the government has decided to make a political opening, but only the power of the people will allow for a solution. The destruction that the 'revolution' (*coup d'État*) brought to the countryside is full of dangers. They expelled people from the country to the cities. We had two million workers here that produced goods for the city without squandering either petrol or gas. These workers possessed two million chickens, two million cows, two million mules and consumed the products of their own individual parcels. All this has been destroyed. After the 'revolution' they created this situation of high prices and scarcity, and all these people are now on the street, dying of hunger, and one squanders petrol, whereas before one used horses and

charcoal. This is what I have to say about
their so-called revolution."

He says this with a harsh voice. Then he
goes on to tell me the history of the peasant
league of Galiléia. He himself is the grandson
of a slave ("My grandmother was worth 200
000 *réis*... I have never learned to read or
write.") He "rebelled" at the age of fifteen, in
1930, when the governor João Pessoa, with
a "socialist tendency," was assassinated.

The peasants were treated worse than
animals. The cattle were at least looked
after. On the plantation, where João Virginio
worked, the people were too poor to pay
for coffins: when someone died they were just
thrown anywhere. Only João Virginio took
care of burying the dead, and he had received
a "poverty attestation" from the commissariat
that gave him the right to free coffins at the town
council. Then they took away this right. He
decided to start a mutual society: peasants would
join forces to pay for coffins. The owner of
the plantation agreed to centralise the funds
and became honorary president. João met with
Zézé Prazeres, a comrade who knew how to
put up a society. Zézé gave him advice. They
called the society of Galiléia 'The Agricultural
and Breeding Society of Plantation Workers
in Pernambuco.' The movement grew. But then,
the son of the patron, a dentist, who wanted
to succeed him, persuaded his father to expel

the associates: "Your society," he said, "is communist. Not on my property. What's more, I want to breed and I need your earth. You get two weeks to clear off." João Virginio went to see the judge of Vitoria. They sent him packing. He went to Recife. Over there a judge told him that the labour code forbade such an expulsion without compensation, and gave him the address of a lawyer, a deputy at the assembly of the state, that could help him. This lawyer's name was Francisco Julião. They spoke the entire night, João Virginio described at length the conditions of the peasants in the plantations. Francisco Julião agreed to defend them. A long juridical battle followed. The battle lasted for eight years, during which the patron repeatedly tried to kill João Virginio through henchmen. He received severe beatings but always ran away. In the end they lost the case. But Julião took it to the assembly of the state. The peasants went all the way to Recife to occupy the seat for two days. The majority of the deputies gave the peasants rights against the owner. Following this vote, the governor expropriated Galiléia and indemnified the owner. Every peasant family got the right to ten hectares.

"Since this time, each of us has lived on our little farms. The government doesn't give us any help. They refuse to construct a road and you have seen how difficult the access to the village is. We have been here for twenty years. We have no comfort, nothing." João Virginio speaks about the times of Arraes as being the sole period when the government took concrete measures to help the peasants. "When Arraes raised the salaries by 300%, one saw for the first time beds and chairs appear in the houses of the peasants: until then, they were too poor to purchase them.

Then came the 'revolution.' I kept hidden here for seven days. After seven days I couldn't escape and was forced to show up. They tortured me for six months and kept me in prison for six years. I have lost one eye, I have lost one ear, and I've got a heart condition. Today, I live on 1100 (160 francs) a month.

If nothing shows up to relieve people, they are going to kill each other. One will see people fight over a paltry yam that somebody has found. The people in the countryside are dying of hunger. It is the worst misery in the world. A guy earns fifty cruzeiros a day, and a kilo of meat costs 120 cruzeiros. How is it possible?"

With the fall of night, the house of João Virginio gently fills up with neighbours who listen and silently approve. He stands up and speaks with his gaze fixed yonder, as if speaking to a large audience.

The next day, I came back with friends and João Virginio wanted us to visit Galiléia. He showed us these places, one after the other,

redolent of events, hopes, blood, massacres.
I thought about Dazhai, the Chinese mountain
village that became a popular commune
famous all over the world, and that I had visited
in 1967. If a popular revolution would have
swept over Brazil, Galiléia would today have
been a centre that delegations from all over
Brazil and the world would visit, where banners
would flap and revolutionary songs sung,
where images and legends would take form.
But only the wind sings in the bare hills, and
the old undefeated man that guides us draws
his authority from a life of struggle.

"The society of Galiléia was founded
over there, in the forest," he says and points
towards the leafy hills. "And here, the hills
have been levelled out to create a club and
a residential complex. Arraes gave us support
to carry out the earthworks." He speaks, with
an enthusiasm that more than fifteen years
haven't shaken, about his trip to Cuba, where
he saw cane cutters transformed by the revolution, and how he, in his turn, wanted to construct arrangements in Galiléia for a new life
similar to the one over there (after his trip,
they started to call him the Cuban, as he spent
so much time describing the island and its
social conquests).

"We wanted to make a cooperative,
a cultural centre, houses, to show that we
could live here without help from the outside.

In 1964 the army came and destroyed everything." He points to the arid landscape,
its small poor houses with their patches of land
that grow onions and cassava, and one under-
stands that for him, this is still the site of the
club, and that the one of the cooperative, and
that he, until his death, will keep the hope that
they will crop up again.

"After the *coup d'État*, the army razed
the seat of our society to the ground. They
demolished one house here, another there, and
yet another there." (He points towards cane
fields without any dwellings.) A bit further, on
the muddy trail: "It was here that we celebrated
when we had won over the plantation owners
in the state assembly. They brought us beef from
all the farms to make a big feast..."

"Then came the coup d'état, and we've
been waiting for fifteen years."

During these fifteen years, João Virginio
made no statements, nor did he invite a single
person from the outside to Galiléia. Now he
speaks again.

As he is walking he names those from
Galiléia who were forced to flee, whom they
tortured, whom they killed.

He takes in the village, the houses that
hang on the side of the valley. He seems to say:
everything is still ahead of us. They wanted to
kill us, but we are still here and, until our last
breath, we will keep the hope.

He makes a gesture toward the horizon.
I imagine other valleys, villages, fields, mountains, forests.

One of the first peasant leagues founded after the one in Galiléia was the one in Acre, three thousand kilometres away, in the middle of the Amazon, on the border with Peru. And for some months, precisely there, in the State of Acre, small-scale peasants have been fighting the *jagunços*, the armed guards that the landowners send out to undertake the expulsions. A deputy from this region has come to Recife and some days ago he explained to me that during recent confrontations in Brasiléia, Boca de Acre, hundreds of workers have taken hold of *jagunços* that were threatening many families. Thus, here and there, downtrodden fires flare up again.

In the midst of the profoundest terror, resistance has been kept alive among the Brazilian peasantry. Now that the social pressure and the economic crisis have weakened the dictatorship, the features, once again, become visible.

It is like a crepuscular state, a still pale morning. A landscape emerges from a very black and long night. One glimpses forms one thought were erased. So, everything was there, moving in the darkness, unknown. One day, we will know.

Photos by
François Manceaux

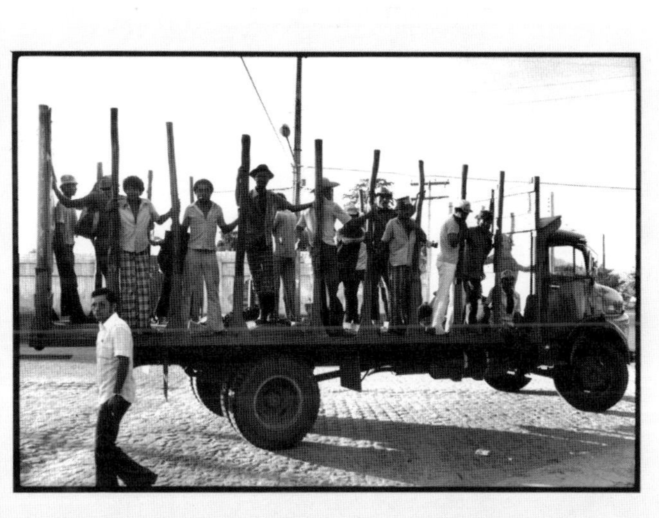

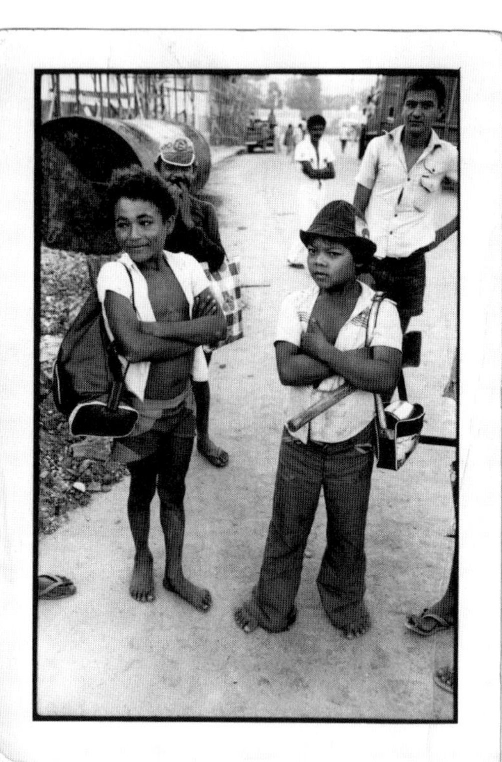

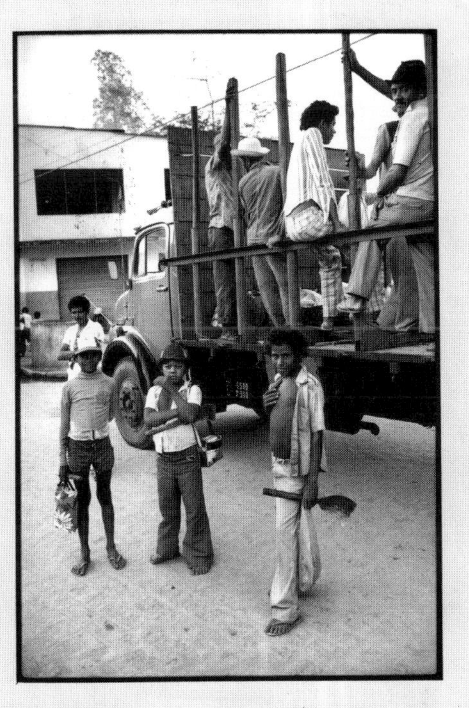

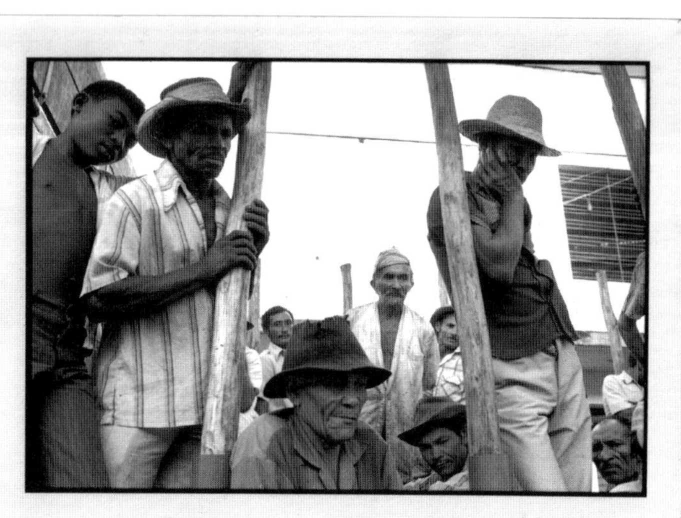

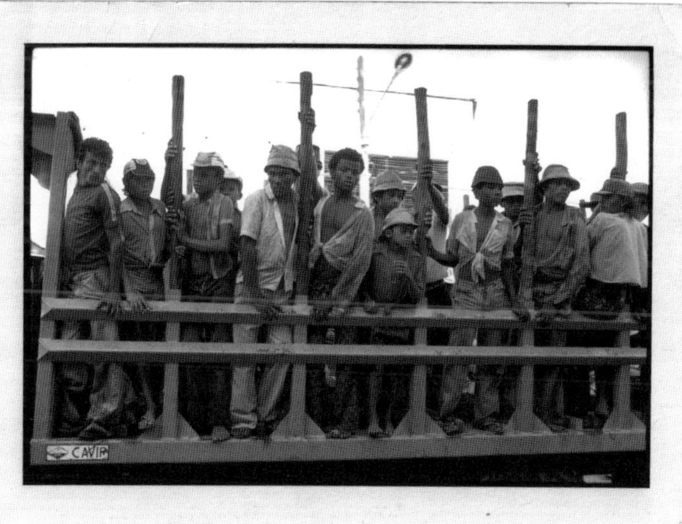

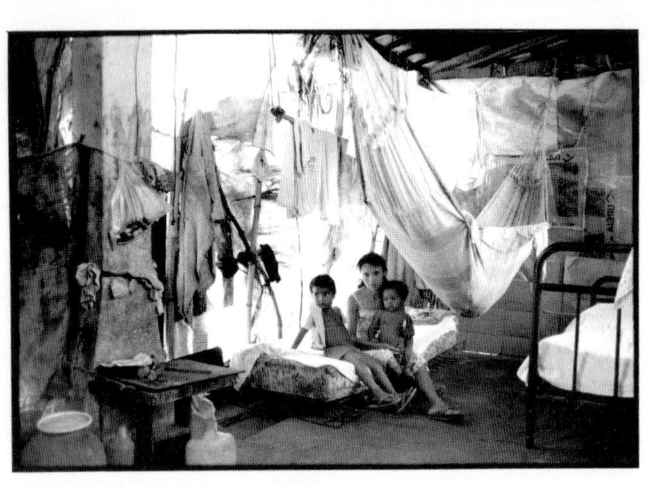

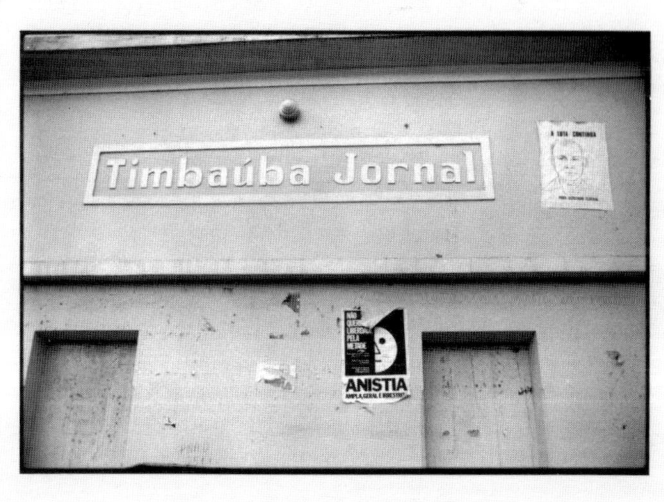

Timbaúba Jornal
A LUTA CONTINUA
NÃO QUER LIBERDADE PELA METADE
ANISTIA
AMPLA, GERAL E IRRESTRITA

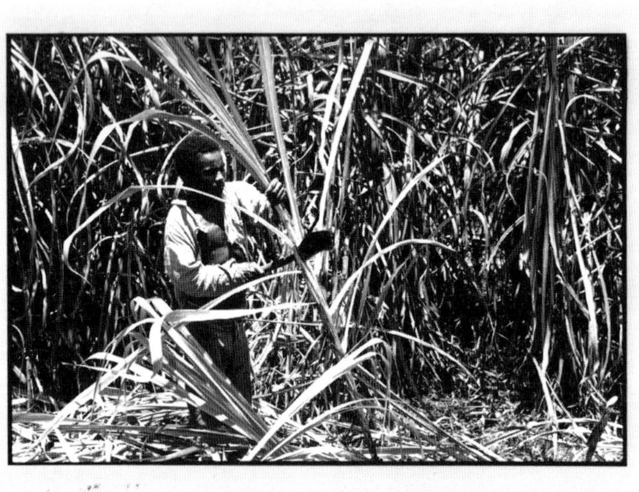

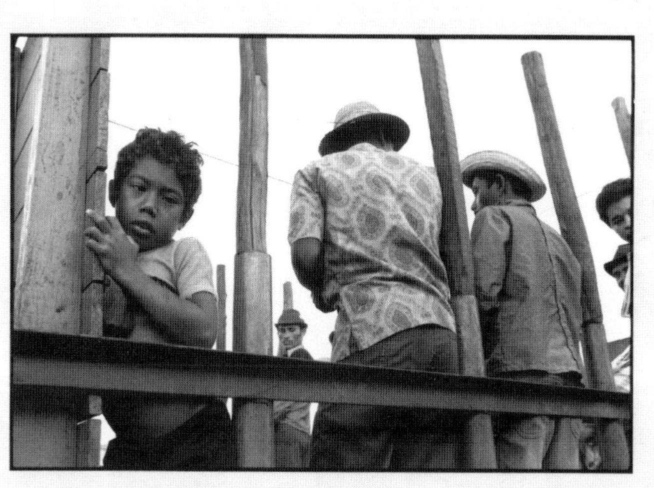

This is an unpublished interview with Robert Linhart retrieved
from his personal archives. We are grateful to Luiz Renato
Martins who made this document available. Unfortunately,
we could not recover the questions of Jean Copans. Neither
Jean nor his brother Richard Copans who directed a docu-
mentary film based on *The Sugar and the Hunger* (Vida Nova,
1985) could recall the content of the interview. Jean Copans
is an anthropologist who describes himself as a "Marxist anti-
imperialist" and who, since the seventies, authored numerous
studies on Africa.

I found myself involved in questions surrounding Brazil
from 1975 onwards, by way of Portugal. In April 1975, I met
Fernando Batista, the new minister of Agriculture in the
Gonçalves government, in Lisboa. He had recently assumed
office and was preparing the implementation of a Land Reform
law. In the Ministry's hallowed halls arose an atmosphere
of improvisation and encampment–temporary governments
followed one after another at an accelerated pace. Batista
requested me to talk about other Land Reforms that I had had
the chance to witness. The Algerian self-management in 1964,
the Chinese people's communes and collectivisation in the
Soviet Union. "You should learn Portuguese and come study
the formation of rural cooperatives with us, on location"
he concluded, following a fairly long discussion on problems
regarding legal statutes, acreages, homogenisation of the
tractor fleet and the relationship between permanent and
seasonal agricultural workers. I started to study Portuguese
and by the summer I returned, ready to undertake the inquiry.
The beginnings were difficult because we expected the
government could fall from one day to another, or we expected
a putsch, or something else no one could really predict, and
because Batista and his colleagues spent their time in ceaseless
meetings. In the end, contact was established with the
Regional Land Reform Centres, a parallel administration
put in place with great haste in order to support, legalise
and organise the movement of agricultural workers
occupying the southern latifundia owners' lands–for this,
the old Salazarist agricultural administration could not be
counted on, and everything was for a while dependent upon
a handful of young intellectuals in the cities, economists,
lawyers, politicised and determined agronomists, who took
on a great deal of work. I participated for some weeks in

the life of the Centres, following the expropriation and organisation of new cooperatives, striving to understand the fast social transformations that modified the relations between land owners, agricultural workers, established or precarious farmers, shepherds, etc. The fall of the Gonçalves government interrupted this work, and my report was stuck in a state of incompleteness – it initiated a debate on the respective roles of salaried agricultural workers and rural small scale land owners in the Portuguese social movement: I was of the opinion that the far left and the Communist Party had based their actions too exclusively on the former while neglecting the latter, who nonetheless made up a large majority of the country's population; only a politics of a much wider class alliance would have been able to preserve the emerging cooperative system in Alentejo from a quick isolation from Portuguese society, and from a counter offensive from the right backed up by the deception of the north and central peasant majority.

Portugal is a small country, with only nine million inhabitants, but I immediately had the feeling of being cast into a much more extensive world, in the middle of upheaval, a world of which I up until then had known almost nothing about. The airports and the cities were flooded by "retornados" (repatriated settlers) from Angola and Mozambique, the conditions of decolonization animated the political class and divided the country, a great deal of Brazilian political refugees found in the linguistic unity the opportunity to blend into a movement of social transformation (others took off to assist in the birth of new Portuguese speaking African states). The collapse of the Portuguese empire appeared to me just as important as what was happening inside the mainland's borders. Actually, at the unexpected end of the empire, the colonising country ended up bloodless and drained, from centuries of overseas adventures, incapable of managing post-colonial transformations, as Great Britain and France had done, and carried on doing – and from here came the abrupt breach that opened in Africa, all the way to the borders of South Africa. I remember the quick succession of news coming from Angola, Mozambique, Timor, Macao, this impression of a mad ship springing leaks all over. The entirety of Lusitanian culture underwent a shock, and this included Brazil, although in a less direct and immediate

manner. It seems to me that the development in Brazil
starting in 1977-78, and later the amnesty of 1979, had one
of its sources here, among many others. In any case, it was
at this time, in this Portuguese maelstrom, that I began
to come across dissident Brazilians.

I had made a first investigative trip to Brazil in 1976-
1977, during which I had studied certain aspects of the country's
industrialisation, the "technology transfer," the "development
hubs" (in particular the petrochemical hub of Camaçari, in
the North-East, in the state of Bahia), and the penetration of
multinational corporations. All of my material was still in
the form of unpublished notes. Later, after the amnesty, I made
another trip to the North-East, right at the time of Miguel
Arraes' return from exile, because the political excitement of
the moment enabled me to get through to the situation in the
rural world in the countryside. I had the intention of making
an inquiry and I said to myself that I, at the same time, could
maybe publish a short report, if I would have enough material
for it. It ended up being something more dense and eventually
took the form of a book–these are things that I did not know in
advance, because I never know what I will see, what I will find,
and for me it is always a surprise when a topic takes on a meaning in itself, as something you can delimit and separate from the
innumerable connections that relate it to the rest of the world
and entangle it within itself. I don't believe that the habitual
splicing of news can create such topics and the most frequent
situation for me is rather an entanglement that does not allow
for them to be produced: things remain thus in the shape
of notes, reports, fragments, with an uncertain attachment to
a country, a theme, a trail.

Why does one inquire a certain question in one place,
and another somewhere else? The technology transfer in
the Algerian East, the sugar cane in the Brazilian North-East,
the land reform in southern Portugal, the petrochemistry
in the region of Marseille? If you ask me, I can not give any
other explanation than the more or less fortuitous details of
encounters, of chain reactions, of opportunities. There is no
ideal spot for the study of such a well-defined question. Once
you penetrate the reality of a country and investigate inside its
system of production you unclog the complexity of the world,
no matter what your point of departure was. Thus, in the

end, what seems important to me, when it comes to choosing
the place for an inquiry, is the actual possibility to inquire,
the knowledge one may gain from people, from language,
the bonds that are being formed in social movements, the
political currents, practices of transformation in sectors
of society. I do not see any other way than to go—or to let
oneself be carried—to the places where one has a chance to
go beyond the simple appearance of things. In the end, everyone inquires in accordance with what they are.

What seems really important to me, in an inquiry,
a story or a case study, is to not search for a pre-established
ideological system. In our times, this becomes a necessary
condition for the survival of thought. If you let yourself be
confined to the meagre ideological alternatives of the French
intellectual milieu, you suffocate. In French ideological production there is a brutal progression of ignorance and a lack
of culture, a triumph of stereotypes (whether it's about the
Third World, Eastern countries or our capitalist societies) to
the extent that I, for my part, do not see any other exit than
a sort of wandering across sequences of phenomena and orders
of heterogeneous reasons, in a constant uncertainty about
the topics that could come into shape. To articulate, when it is
possible, fragments of reality. To choose, for what is confused
or unknown, to silence, or only to point out the confusion,
or manifest ignorance. I believe that the intellectual who
explains the world to his audience in one go has no future.
Or, if he has one, it is a social function for which I do not feel
concerned, and to which I do not adhere. A function of noise
in the system of centralised intoxication that has become so
essential for social peace, a function of the production of
pathetic "cultural" objects to keep running the business of this
flourishing part of the tertiary.

It seems to me that it is urgent for people, who
at the moment have a standpoint to the left, to reconstruct
a perception, that is to say something much larger than
a repertoire of analyses and a "political line." The succession
of ideological reversals, collapses, trends, brief orthodoxies,
have ended up in a sort of saturation point, of general cancel-
lation, which has the effect that, if one does not find a language quickly enough, or several credible, audible languages,
in which to speak about political and social issues, they become

something that will purely and simply wither and disappear from the scene for the majority of people (they will of course always remain available for reduced consumption, between professionals, ever more limited by implicit codes, that, through the amplification game of newspapers, and the audiovisual, once again will seem to massively occupy the terrain when they have become nothing but an empty form, the exterior sign of the recognition of a caste, busy with everything but that which they pretend to talk about. How then, did the Latin language— so alive, spoken by millions of people, capable of transmitting feelings, love, hate, the language of porters, of sailors, of soldiers, of politicians, of writers, of prostitutes, of lunatics, of bankers—become the frozen code of rite, of Mass, of feudal command, of medical prescription, of alchemical treatises, excluding all spontaneous communication between ordinary people? Cultures and languages are mortal and this small milieu still believes itself to be communicating with the entire world, when all it does, being already imprisoned and isolated, is to soliloquize on the edges of nothingness).

Wooden language, ideological simplifications, media hypes, and abrupt amnesias from the sixties and seventies— what is the point of citing them once more, when the very idea of enumeration already provokes weariness: we really have a problem when it comes to the survival of communication around all these questions. You can always say the problem lies in the form, but I believe it to lie in the depth. If we want vibrant political cultures and methods of analysis to subsist here—I would not call it a "sociology" but a culture of living social analysis—we have to invent a style, several styles, and ways of functioning, a credibility, to find a way to transmit (and to receive) knowledge and feelings that were diminished in the French intellectual milieu's attempts and failures—which without a doubt is also in the course of its fragmentation and professionalised rigidity, connected to the powerful development of capitalism in all the sectors of cultural production in the last fifteen years.

There is, in our culture, an outright refusal to understand cultural systems and civilisations other than our own, a fact from which one can derive the grotesque functioning of stereotypes and simplifications, this daily gruel that we are being

served disguised as "news" from the world. All countries in the
Third World, all countries in the East, have complex societies,
and the complexity of actual mechanisms and of systems of
representation in these societies, the perpetually moving
relationships between the social forces and the functioning
of the modes of production, make up a whole lot more than
the more or less backwards, more or less famished, more or
less robotized, far away mass of people, that we are presented.
Whatever the apparent quantity of given information,–and
sometimes you don't skimp on expenses–, it all comes down
to a certain number of schemes that very easily can be compared to the schemes of the 19th century, to colonial literature. This, fundamentally, does not seem particularly
remarkable to me, insofar as I find that exactly those relations
that our societies uphold with those in the Third World (with
what we these days name the Third World) are reproducing
many aspects of the relations that existed in the 19th century.
If we take, for example, the debt mechanism, that has become
a key mode of exploitation in many Third World countries
(Brazil, Zaire, Indonesia, and many others), it is comparable to
what was done, in the 19th century, to China, Turkey, Persia
and many others, who were drained of blood without being
official colonies. Currently, Zaire is so indebted that different
bank consortiums and European institutions directly handle
the management of certain sectors of public finances and
administration–not to mention the mining empires, enclaves
and concessions of all kinds.

The IMF intervened in Peru as well, to dictate the details of
political economy, and if this mechanism is not directly at play
in Brazil (although the threat has already been raised, even
by some of the politicians in power), it is only because there
is a strong military regime that directly takes charge of what
a European bank consortium or an international financial insti-
tution would have handled. In any case, one comes to the same
result through the ideological domination of local "elites" and
diverse methods of blackmailing and arm-twisting, as through
a direct takeover. See Milton Friedman in Chile. The politics
of Antônio Delfim Netto in Brazil (the "model" of food industry
export and uncontrolled industrialisation) play so perfectly
into the hands of multinational corporations by opening the
world market, that there is no need for institutional controllers

in situ: the result is still the same and the appearance of
national independence is withheld. There is a "*comprador*"
economical thinking, as one used to talk about the comprador
bourgeoisie, a dependent bourgeoisie, totally committed
to the interests of the imperial or colonial powers. Today,
the quick circulation of information and the ways of life of
the dominant classes, or the ways of life in general, make up
unified networks of bankers, of speculators, of military, of
politicians, of newspapermen, etc. that constitute the global
milieu in which multinational corporations develop, the fish
water – shark's water. Ipanema, an uptown neighbourhood
in the southern part of Rio de Janeiro (where one finds large
luxury hotels and joggers on the mosaic-decorated alleys
that run along the beach and the "*lagoa*", the city's inland
lake), is closer, when it comes to appearance and customs,
to San Francisco than to the "*favelas*" and the "*conjuntos
habitacionais*" (social housing) in the north of Rio. Without
a doubt closer to the outposts of plunder. But here as well as
there, you find the same satiated fifty-something guys, the
same busy businessmen, the same idle young sportsmen, the
same smooth cover-girls, the same intellectuals engaging
in analysis, the same relaxation coaches, and parasites of all
sorts. Power and squandering. The power to squander, surely
even more spectacular in Latin America than in North America.
In 1976, I was struck by the osmosis of the military devices
in Bahia. Received at a senior officer's place, the brother of
a friend, I discovered the Brazilian version of the marines.
Panamanian anti-guerilla school, training camps in California.
American furnishings, chromolithographs depicting American
landscapes, photos with American dedications (friends,
promotors, colleagues), American decorations. "Dad, when
will we go back to Los Angeles?" And to designate the
winter holidays that occurred at the time, no one used the word
"*Natal*" (in Portuguese), but exclusively "Christmas." The great
topic of conversation, between the megalomaniac delusions
about the exploitation of the Amazon that in short order
would make Brazil the richest country in the world and the
happy memories from the massacres of "*guerrilleros*" and
peasants on the borders of Bolivia, was the recent election
of Carter, the demagogue who sent his children to the same
schools as the "negroes" and who had chosen a Black man
to represent the United States in the United Nations. These

Brazilian military men from Rio occupied the Northeastern
territories as if they represented an outpost of civilization
in the wilderness. (The State of Bahia is the heart of African
culture in Brazil, and the primary historical centre for
the deportation of enslaved Africans; the soldiers of these
white officers were almost all Black; and the officers maintained no relations with them apart from their howling of
commands and their use of them as servants.) Luckily, they
had their sweet memories of the mainland and the neighbourhood comforts, this preserved island of "the American way
of life," to keep them warm.

A country like Brazil currently owes an external debt
of more than fifty billion dollars (no one knows, as a matter
of fact, the exact sum, and I've heard estimations that exceed
sixty billion dollars). An unbelievable amount. During one
year you would have to find seven billion in interest alone, five
billion due in capital repayment, a certain amount of complementary loans become absolutely necessary, in all something
like fifteen billion dollars. The most efficient means to find
such a sum? Sell everything: land, minerals, foodstuffs, soy,
sugar, coffee, manufactured goods when possible, etc. Delfim
Netto's plan to make Brazil a substantial producer in the
food industry, turning more and more towards export, leads
to a paradoxical and tragic situation: a country, very rich
in agricultural land, all of which is diverted to export or even
the transformation of crops into gasoline (the politics of
"biomass" that already uses sugar and is now heading for
manioc and other crops), at the cost of food crops and the
nourishment of the population. The export of agricultural
goods should in theory allow the financing of the "centres
of industrialisation" but we see how these centres themselves
function as systems of drainage, of job losses and of the
extension of slums; anyhow, these "centres," apart from seeing
their production correspondingly absorbed by debt repayment, are frenzied consumers of currencies through the
implementation of foreign technology, and do nothing else
but accelerate the spiral effect they were meant to break
(it is the manifest mistake of the so called "import substitution"
policy). The pumping of debt is quite similar to the way in
which the great imperialist and colonial powers of the 19th
century overtook various countries that fell under their heavy
blow. When the mechanisms of exploitation are as similar as

this, it is no surprise to find ideological attitudes and systems
of representation to be very similar. Even the so called
"Human Rights" policies and the great renewal of the idea of
the missionary doctor and the charitable West, bringing light
and relief to the savages, takes us back to the epoch of the
colonial powers' good civilising consciousness, when gunboats,
expeditionary forces and scorched-earth policies were accom-
panied by images of pious conversion, vaccination or the liberation of slaves. The presentation of the Third World as
a jumble of savagery is the necessary ideological aspect of all
operations of takeover and dispossession.

First through colonisation and other ways of plundering, and
today through the "development policy" and the "industrialisation of the Third World," one observes the establishment
of a modern hunger, a corollary to the plague (*gangrene*) of
export monocultures. That is to say, hunger can not be charac-
terised as the unfortunate lingering on of past situations that
we are in the process of overcoming, but, on the contrary,
as the very extension and evolving outcome of "development,"
that everywhere takes the form of a brutal or slow destruction
of the earlier productive and nutritive balance, even if this
balance took place in poverty. It is the hunger of precarious
employment, of proletarianization and sub-proletarianization,
of urban nutritional monotony, it is the hunger of displaced
populations being subjected to successive shocks, dependent
on the global market's dreadful requirements—what they call
"the food weapon," whose victims can already be counted in
the millions. All over the world nutritional deficiency is pro-
gressing, becoming the principal instrument for a definitive
mutilation of entire populations, entire generations—the
throwback of an entire part of the human species to a status
of sub-humanity. It is a more malicious method of destruction
than the old hunger, the "traditional famine," if I may say so,
as it embeds itself rigorously into the capitalist organisation on
a global scale. Before the shock of the colonies, the spreading
of monocultures and industrial centres, a certain balance was
respected even within the undernutrition-zones: agriculture-
breeding-complementarity, crop diversity, the combination of
mountain and lowland agriculture, grazing on fallow land and
natural fertilisers, parsimonious but relatively shared usage
of water, balanced eating habits. In the case of Algeria, it has

been uncovered how French colonisation, by monopolising the most fertile lowlands and in so doing pushing back the *fellahs* to the foothills, created two separate zones, the "traditional" and the modern, at the price of genuine destruction, a progression of erosion, the end of exchange between lowland growing and mountain breeding, the drying out and sterilisation of whole regions, condemned to become enormous islands of poverty. A historical trauma accelerated by the war's massive deportations, and which, twenty years after independence, is far from erased, even though agricultural self-management and agrarian Revolution have been implemented. In Mozambique, in Brazil we find similar things: colonisation, capitalism and latifundia have profoundly disrupted the natural balances.

In the overwhelming majority of cases, what Third World hunger means is first and foremost the nutritive impact that all these upheavals have in the domains of soil occupation, land use, and finally habitat, because we know that the ultimate end (at least for the moment) of this process is the spreading of slums: once the majority of the land has been monopolised, once the monoculture directed toward the export has invaded everything, once the colonisers, or the foreign firms, or the local landowners have pushed back the small scale peasants, which for them is the final phase, only the abandoning of the peasant status and the bunching up around large cities, under well-known conditions of the destruction of familial and social structures, remains. The impact on nutrition: everything now depends upon low-wage work, where one salary can be shared by ten, twenty, thirty people. Food can only be found in the shops, in exchange for these meagre cash incomes. All of that which is called the subsistence system has practically disappeared for these populations. As, at the same time, the extension of monocultures leads to a heavy price increase in foodstuffs, now coming from much farther away or being imported from abroad (which after all is a paradox when it comes to fertile rural areas), the population is limited to extreme nutritional scarcity: flour staple foods, occasionally rice and beans, to the exclusion of milk, meat, fish, many vitamins, and whole foods for the children. This leads to a situation where people can have their bellies full without having assured the nutrition needed to reproduce and to develop vital functions (especially irreversible is the

damage to the neurons in young children's brains). This is the
major, massive and tragic, shape of hunger today. Some figures
from the UN estimate the number of people that are in a state
where their nutrition is too poor to assure normal functioning
of the organism, the nervous system and the brain, to be
as high as 700 million, globally. This figure is obviously very
approximate, but one sees immediately that we are dealing
with a problem of overwhelming magnitude. In entire regions,
the physical characteristics are modified from generation
to generation under this unfailing pressure: decreased height,
psychological weakness, stunting of psychomotor skills, etc.
This is, by the way, why campaigns on starvation, when presented
exclusively as localised famines (following wars or droughts)
are insufficient and sometimes even damaging. Emergency aid,
such as food packages, can be useful or even completely
indispensable in specific cases, where they can be used to save
lives that are endangered in the short term, but it obviously
does not solve the problem of the immense majority of the mal-
nourished in the Third World – to sprinkle different communities with flour sacks has, in general, no other effect other
than to disrupt local circuits through speculation and to
accelerate the destruction of what is left of local agriculture,
while spreading parasitism and dependence. In Algeria,
while working in the Agriculture Ministry in 1964, I heard
a vigorous denouncement – and in my opinion rightly so – of
the food aid lobby. India was given as an example, where
the pressure from ship-owners through government channels
had forced to accept the unwanted "gift" of American grain
surplus, unwanted because the charges of the transportation
were to be paid by the receiving country: the food was for
free but the freight cost was an enormous affair and it was
estimated that the final result of the operation aggravated the
situation in India, for the benefit of big American capitalist
companies, under the guise of "assistance."

The only way to fight against the massive hunger,
incorporated as malnutrition, is to put an end to the general development of the export monocultures, to systems
of indebtedness, to the rural exodus, thus ultimately to
the global relations between the countries of the Third
World and the countries that exploit their riches and their
populations. Problems in the overall balance of production,
land, consuming patterns and social life will not be solved

with emergency aid or aid circuits. Nor can we imagine
that any large-scale change might intervene in the Third
World without a transformation of our own societies,
as the systems are too deeply interlinked.

In the book, I talk about the doctor and nutritionist Nelson
Chaves from Pernambuco. For a long time, he has been leading
a fierce struggle against hunger, and he disseminates tonnes
of precise data about its progression, its transformations
and its effects. There are of course people, who, like him, are
directly confronted with this problem in their roles as doctors:
the major medical condition in North-Eastern hospitals is
starvation; the major cause of infant mortality is starvation.
From the North-East of Brazil, now spread all over the world,
come some of the undoubtedly most well-known books on
the issue: *The Geography of Hunger* (1946) and *The Geopolitics
of Hunger* (1952) by Josué de Castro. These books were
published more than thirty years ago, and are unfortunately
still utterly current on many points. In the regions most
affected by malnutrition, there is a small intelligentsia that is
more directly engaged with this reality, a milieu of doctors,
biologists, economists, agronomists, that are aware of the
situation and are trying to change it—through relations with
authorities, the FAO [Food and Agriculture Organization of
the United Nations], through local initiatives, etc., or by trying
to alert public opinion, or by more radical actions, there you
certainly have something to quickly be politicised by... But for
a lot of intellectuals, who live in regions that are affected to
a lesser extent or whose professional and ideological activity
lack immediate relevance to malnutrition, things are a lot
more vague. More generally speaking, this causes problems in
Brazilian intellectuals' relationship with their own country—as is
the case with intellectuals in many Third World countries. One
of the components of this situation is precisely the imperialist
countries' cultural domination, the power exercised by their
university institutions, their research system, and their "intellectual giants." Their professors of higher education and
researchers have generally studied abroad, and remain very
marked by their background. In Rio, people are on the lookout
for Parisian intellectual trends, "events" that shake the small
world of our literature, philosophy or psychoanalyst schools,
people are looking to the tendencies in American economical

or sociological thought, and rush to conferences with Foucault
or Galbraith. And those who produce cultural objects first
and foremost aspire to have them appreciated by European
and North American audiences. The extroversion of the culture
of the "elites" is as strong as the extroversion of the economy.
Yet Brazil presents a linguistic unity (the Portuguese, official
language, is also a language spoken by the people), which is
not the case in many Third World countries.

Thus, in the big urban and cultural centres, Rio,
São Paulo, and in the South-East region more generally, the
relationship that the intelligentsia maintains with Northeastern
problems is quite similar to those that an intellectual in Paris
can maintain with those in Sahel: there is a far away colonial
dependence, known more or less by readers; people who work
with it — the IBRD [International Bank for Reconstruction
and Development], emergency plans, etc. — in general one talks
less about it, except for when there's a drought... The tragic
situation in the North-East is not common knowledge. Still,
it is fair to say that there have existed small active groups that
are aware of the situation in the North-East, and who publish
studies, and strive to alert the public about it. For example
the São Paulo CEBRAP group [the Brazilian Center for Analysis
and Planning], with Francisco de Oliveira and Paul Singer.
But they are in the minority. One also has to keep in mind
the extreme fragmentation of Brazilian society, the large gap
that separates rich and poor, and the marginalisation of vast
fractions of the population. The military dictatorship has, after
all, by no means loosened its pressure on the popular masses,
even though it has loosened some of its pressure on the bourgeoisie and allowed a certain amount of political freedom and
freedom of expression. The death squads continue to operate
on a large scale (there were a thousand deaths in greater
Rio in 1980), but its current targets are the "common rights,"
the inhabitants of the favelas — the shanty towns where the
"dangerous classes" can be found. Strikes remain dangerous
operations that imply exposure to violence from the police,
para-police and all sorts of militias. Recently, an important
union leader was murdered in São Paulo, simply because
he was found picketing. It is very common that pickets are
attacked, and striking workers beaten up. The legislation
that strikes are subjected to makes it possible to declare almost
all strikes illegal, and violence immediately follows. All this

contributes to the difficulty in establishing liaisons with the
working class and the peasantry. During the darkest years,
the progressive part of the Church played a very important
role in maintaining contact with the most oppressed masses,
and it continues to play this role today, especially for
the "grass-root communities."

43 Years Later:
The Relevance of *The Sugar and the Hunger*[1]
Luiz Renato Martins

Translated from the Portuguese
by Emillio Sauri

Prologue
in the Form of Questions

What is the relevance today of this critical essay—a work emblematic of an era, titanic (despite being as small as a David facing Goliath)—on class struggle and the intensification of inequality, within the context of economic expansion under late and accelerated modernization? A deep surgical cut, in fact, into a country then considered a tiger of agile and successful industrialization by capitalist standards—something, certainly, very different from the evident state of things today: that of an old tiger infected by the plague of the ultraright (perhaps kept in check, but not defeated). In sum, what does Linhart's inquiry bring to our current moment?

And, especially, in times of recession and crisis, what is its critical force against the defence of economic growth as general panacea—a widespread idea among economists close to investors, but also among the leaders of the government in Brazil recently elected in the name of democracy and the fight against hunger in October 2022? At this point, what is its warning about hunger-fighting programs which, with aid as its only goal, fail to consider the role of hunger as a strategy of domination?

Hunger:
From Colonial to Modern Forms

To apprehend, first, the critical and creative originality of *The Sugar and The Hunger*'s intervention, and, then, its contemporary relevance, let us focus on those features salient to its first publication (in *Le Monde*, Paris, on February 3, 1980, p. VI; and, as a book published by Éditions de Minuit the same year). With a thought-provoking pace and markedly visual content, *The Sugar and The Hunger* saw the reciprocal determination between the expansion of the monoculture

of sugar and the phenomenon of mass hunger as a product
of capitalism; therefore, as something modern, rational, and
functional to the reproductive logic of capital.

It is a well-known fact in Brazil that the cultivation
of sugarcane represented, within the colonial framework of
Portuguese America, the first step towards the establishment
of an export-oriented manufacturing economic order. After
the immediate fury of accumulation following the lethal introduction of colonisation, based on plunder or mere extractive
practices (enslavement of indigenous peoples and expropriation
of their land and goods, extraction of pau-brasil wood, etc.),
colonial economic activity, without ceasing to be despotic,
took root and gained a certain complexity. The production
of value reached a new level, through the organisation of
sugarcane cultivation and the manufacturing process in the
mills—producers of a compost processed for exportation—all
of which demanded a double articulation with international
trade: the massive importation of enslaved individuals brought
from Africa by the slave trade, forming the primary source of
labour and labour's appropriation; and the related production
for export of a commodity of scarce local consumption, sugar.[2]

It is no surprise to anyone observing the history of the
inequality inherent to the Brazilian social formation founded
on the latifundium, that hunger and food shortages became
widespread throughout the colonial process amidst the dis-
organisation of indigenous economies of gathering and subsistence in favour of monoculture and its intensified repro-
duction by the inequality that slave labour engendered.

Taking dehumanisation and hunger as basic elements
of the colonial plantation, *The Sugar and The Hunger* focuses
on the more contemporary and decisive finding that, in
addition to being a deliberate act, the articulation between
monoculture and mass hunger took on an unprecedented
scale as a result of new measures imposed by the civil-
military dictatorship from April 1964 onward, and even
more so after AI-5.[3]

This is a shift, coupled with the deepening of despo-
tism, to restructuring the workforce and raising the rate of
exploitation; a process further accelerated shortly thereafter
with the production of ethanol linked to the expansion of
the automotive sector. In this sense, and although without
mentioning the concept, one might see *The Sugar and*

The Hunger as participating in the set of studies (mostly Latin American, but not only) that made the concept of *super-exploitation* part of international debate.[4]

From the Concrete
to the General

Viewed within a broader context and in dialectical continuity with other works by Linhart like *L'Établi* [The Assembly Line, 1978] and subsequent studies (many in collaboration with the sociologist Danielle Linhart, his sister) on labour relations in factories, the political crux of the matter examined in *The Sugar and The Hunger* encompasses the vast restructuring (led by capital) of labour and domination patterns–a restructuring defined in the mid-1970s that led to the establishment of a new capitalist cycle of accumulation (the one we are in now).

What role did the political organisation of workers and patterns of domination play in the productive transition from the previous capitalist cycle of accumulation (Fordist-Taylorist) to the current one? How and by what means did the capitalist system, after piling up a series of setbacks–namely, a decline in profitability linked to the accumulated growth of the wage bill during the postwar period and afterwards; social and political conflict, which led to pre-revolutionary conditions and confrontations with bourgeois hegemony (1968); the creation of OPEC and a related rise in oil prices (1973) shaking the unilateral power of core economies–how, in short, could capitalism renew itself in the transition from the 1960s to the 1970s under such conditions? What did this entail on the production lines and in the general forms of labour immediately after?[5]

In brief, within such a context of economic upheavals and crises of hegemony, what is the role and value of investigating the particularity of the restructuring of labour relations in the sugarcane agroindustry–which took place between 1964 and 1979 in the North-East region of Brazil–for the larger discussion about the systemic redefinition of the current mode of exploitation?

157

Hunger:
A Strategic Goal

Thus, returning to the concrete particularity highlighted
by the title (the link between sugar and hunger), the analysis
of the sugarcane agroindustry also calls for, dialectically,
that of the related term: the necro-industry of hunger production, standing, from the beginning, in direct relation to
monoculture. In this sense, mass hunger, previously perceived
as by-product and sporadic fact, was reproduced during
the modernisation of the sugarcane agroindustry coupled with
the development of the automotive sector, updating itself,
in functional terms as a result of planning as well as a cause:
namely, of wage compression, of increases in productivity
and profit rates; and therefore, serving to deter working class
political organisation by inducing chronic illnesses linked
to starvation (as we will see below).

In summary, *The Sugar and The Hunger*'s thesis is
that mass hunger, as a factor of domination, played a decisive
role in the new agroindustry economy, based on flexible
or *precarious* labour, to use a current term. See, for example,
the testimony of an unidentified engineer, in the key chapter
'Back to Recife' discussed below. As for the laboratory-
like nature of the experiment in Pernambuco in 1964 and
subsequent years, captured by *The Sugar and The Hunger*'s
moving gaze (to emphasise its cinematic visual dimension),
it is up to the reader to decide. Nevertheless, it is important
to note: the socio-economic experiment analysed by
Linhart predates by several years (and on a smaller scale,
certainly) that of the neoliberal laboratory[6] set up in
Santiago de Chile, in September 1973, under the management of the Chicago Boys.[7]

In fact, the field study conducted by Linhart in 1979
in the state of Pernambuco tracking the impact of the civil-
military coup in 1964 on the organisation of workers gathers
evidence of the means by which the strategic connection
between agroindustry and hunger renewed itself (means, by
the way, which, since then, have worsened and brought about
various others harms, including the tragic self-doping of day
workers, so-called *boias-frias*,[8] to increase individual tonnage,
in a sinister reenactment [now anabolized by the drug] of the
Stalin-Stakhanovist production model serving [now as before]
the cause of late and accelerated development).[9]

However, before delving into the productive sugar-hunger symbiosis analysed by *The Sugar and The Hunger*, let's examine its strategic operative premise. This premise is central to the book's impact today: the nexus between production and death is associated in the text with two thought-images (*Denkbild*, following the meaning that Walter Benjamin gave the term): the concentration camp and the nuclear bomb.

It is hard to imagine more macabre and malign undertakings in the twentieth century. As baleful cases go, they only find analogues in previous centuries in colonisation and slavery. Used as metaphors, they function as impactful figures that cannot fit into a hasty statement. They call for caution, care, and an almost cinematic weaving; and, in this particular case, they require editing skills, so as not to overshadow the facts, obscuring the sugar and hunger nexus. This explains, as I see it, the evident simplicity and functionality of other discursive articulations (in the mould of cinematographic discourse ...). This also explains the care taken to anchor the two maximalist metaphors in a context and tie the one to the other, both borrowed from the Brazilian debate.

For now, let us note that these two sinister forms of massive and lethal techniques stem from historical and technological frameworks that are related, or even reciprocally determined. They necessarily share a common active principle or element: an assertion of racial supremacy. In fact, given the scope of the device, the target selected for the nuclear bomb presupposes the operational objective of mass extermination, forcibly measured by criteria of racial supremacy. From this perspective, in addition to the juxtaposition of the two inventions – and as horrible as it is to find planning and "improvement" in the matter, the evidence of "technical progress" stands out. Indeed, compared to the management of death in extermination camps, the practice of genocide through the invention of the bomb evolved in terms of automatism and range, in scale and speed. The invention of the nuclear bomb thus brought about a technical-productive leap in terms of a capitalist expansion,[10] which views technology as a strategic resource against the *dangerous* (from capital's own perspective) dependence on human labour-power.

Returning to the figurative schema referring to the industry of death, the first "thought-image" used by *The Sugar and The Hunger* to glimpse the sugar-hunger nexus, is that of the *mega* concentration camp. It summarises the fate of the North-East region (hereafter referred to simply as "Nordeste," following colloquial usage in Brazil). The second image is that of the *dirty bomb*, depicting the effect of mass hunger. This metaphor, borrowed from poetry, alludes to the pathological scourge, discussed below, of diarrhoea within the victimised body.

Objective Universality and (Figurative) Keys
to the Universal in the Particular

Undoubtedly stemming from intense emotions, the adoption of the two figures also proves historically objective and necessary. With his grandparents having disappeared in the extermi--nation camps, Robert Linhart could see in the impact of mass hunger on the *nordestinos* (the people from the North-East) similarities with the experience of the survivors of Nazi death camps.

In situations of empathy and affection, the work of attention and imagination hastens. Perhaps from this arises the spontaneous eruption throughout the narrative of sensations that, I gather, came to Linhart from a vivid desire to portray the unnameable; a desire soon translated into scenes captured during his investigation. These manifestations compose a narrative flow that involves and marks the reading, persistently imbuing it with the outline of figures, albeit fleeting. This technique recalls the effect of handheld shots in several films from Brazilian Cinema Novo; films, it should be noted, that Linhart followed with special attention.[11]

Such "messianic" manifestations or illuminations (in the sense of Benjamin's last essay, written in 1940 under Nazi occupation[12]) constitute syntheses in the form of visual insights that spring up within the critical and scientific vein that governs *The Sugar and The Hunger*'s investigative leitmotif—constructed, in general, from data, studies, eyewitness accounts, and testimonials from collaborators. In fact, as the son of a Polish Jewish couple that emigrated to France before the war and went underground during the occupation, Robert was born in 1944, in a country taken over by Nazi troops, from which his parents escaped thanks to the courage of a couple of "fair-minded" farmers who gave them refuge and protection in the rural South of France, despite constant surveillance and harassment.

By combining the apprehension of determinations and of fortuitous arrangements, or, in other words, of the universal and the contingent, Linhart's attention and vision are certainly nourished by his family history, but this doesn't make them idiosyncratic or untimely expressions, since, in fact, they bear objective bases and demonstrate a rationale. The scenes under focus, despite being bound up in the geographic peculiarity of the Brazilian *Nordeste*, belong to the global system of capitalist *ratio*, whose concrete unity and homogeneity, despite the particularities, allow for the reading of its universality, irrespective of geographic inscription, following the dialectic of class conflict.

At the same time, this systemic dimension, which certainly comprises abstract and formal schemas, requires critical and concrete exactness, that is, sensitive and embodied precision, to offer a dialectical and effective vision of the concrete and particular phenomenon. To this end, Linhart resorts to—precisely in order to achieve the direct effect of a presence inherent to the feeling grounded in concreteness—the two specific figurative keys mentioned earlier: that of the *concentration camp*, as the double and the synthetic equivalent of the region, and the figure of the *dirty bomb*, as an allegorical allusion to the nuclear bomb; both, crucial metaphors that function as imagistic condensations of historical experiences (hence their objectivity).

Both metaphors stem from the Brazilian debate; thus, they have concrete ties to local history and the sensible universe of their mnemonic experiences, without neglecting world-historical experiences. The lawyer and founding leader of the Ligas Camponesas (Peasant Leagues), who was also a congressman deposed by the dictatorship, Francisco Julião described the Nordeste as an immense *concentration camp*.[13] The poet and art critic Ferreira Gullar is the author of the metaphor of the *dirty bomb* in a poem of the same title.[14]

The *dirty bomb*, as a weapon of mass destruction—but of a broader spectrum by targeting, more than a territory, an entire class—manifests itself through chronic diarrhoea, a consequence of hunger lodged in the viscera from breastfeeding on; fate of the class subjected, after the civil-military coup of 1964, not just to the prohibition against the right to organise, but also to the seizure of the right to cultivate the small parcel of land around their homes; ancestral right that

provided each worker with the possibility of practicing, to
a minimal degree, "subsistence farming," as well as of engaging
in the raising of chickens, pigs, goats, rabbits, etc.

From Confiscation to Diarrhoea:
A Class Logic

Beyond confiscating homes, this nefarious and heinous
dispossession also brought with it the suppression of the
peasant' main source of nutrition. This confiscation further
led to subsequent social injuries, with multiple consequences
due to the spread in urban areas of problems arising from
pauperisation and the eradication of self-subsistence in
rural areas. This gave rise to continuous streams of migrants
leaving rural zones, resulting in a growing belt of homeless
residents around cities, where those displaced from rural
areas seek refuge.[15]

With these calamities, moreover, an extensive
and widespread increase of living costs and food shortages
was also established, along with a grave nutritional
deficiency inherent in industrially processed foods; while
misery and hunger inevitably became a prevalent and
growing reality in cities, particularly for those without
money or jobs.

In brief, such measures served to coerce acceptance
of low and insufficient wages, which lead to the confluence
of survival and chronic hunger. In this way, like the ban –
described by Marx[16] and other authors – against workers
collecting production leftovers (woodchips discarded by ship-
yards, fabric scraps thrown out by tailors, etc.) in nineteenth-
century Germany and England, pauperization and malnutrition were organised and planned. In this case, they function
as specific additives for the growth of the supply of labour –,
much like the use of chemical fertilisers aiming to increase
the agricultural production of large landed estates, despite
various risks to public health.

Furthermore, diarrhoea, an effect triggered by daily
hunger, weakens the working class from within, decimating
both physical health and subjectivity. Acting preventively,
it incapacitates the worker from the extra effort needed for
organising politically.

Linhart borrowed the idea of the *dirty bomb* from a poem recited by one of his collaborators while driving back to Recife. Thus, the decisive poetic form – for the title, as well as for life in the form of horror – appears here not as *ex machina* solutions, but as a form found in the immanent dynamics of the story, in this case, amid a description of the landscape. In this way, *The Sugar and The Hunger* manages to incorporate and pass from one narrative tempo to another (description, testimony, pre-existing findings and critical constructs, geographic and historical data, comments, reflexions, etc.), giving the reader a rare sense of presence that neither deviates from nor contradicts, but rather confers concreteness and a defined focus to the historical understanding of the whole.

How might we explain this fact? I see no other way other than invoking extraverbal devices and ways of narrating. For locating the narrative always within a context, listening, selection, and montage constitute architectural and cinematic virtues that function as the narrative mainstays of *The Sugar and The Hunger*.

Thus, the interviews with professors Nelson Chaves, a nutritionist at the Maternal-Infant Institute of the Pernambuco's hospital in Recife; with economist Maria da Conceição Tavares from ECLAC [UN's Economic Commission for Latin America and the Caribbean], conducted four years earlier, in 1976; and with an unnamed engineer, held in Paris shortly before the trip, play a decisive role in providing a historical perspective on mass hunger and socio-economic inequality, exposing step by step how both serve domination.

An active and attentive reading of *The Sugar and The Hunger*'s creative and critical practices makes it possible to detect how the structures inherent to the colonial process, and modernised within the framework of the imbalances and disproportions inherent to the current regime of productive expansion associated with dependency (explained by the ECLAC economist), converge historically, blending archaic and modern temporalities in their determinations, in such a way as to produce today what Linhart calls an "immense rotting"[17] of nations and classes condemned to asymmetry.

Wide Shots, Close-ups,
and Montage

The narrative development of *The Sugar and The Hunger* is basically structured around distinct diegetic units that are, for the most part, eminently visual. Guided by parameters of historical understanding and the dialectic of classes grasped through dialogues with members of the Brazilian intelligentsia, such sequences function as general and objective landmarks that reflexively enhance the description of scenes and details of human figures—these, presented *perceptively* or in close-ups, and in an organic visual connection with the surroundings, distinguished both as scenography and meaningful historical *habitat*.

There is, therefore, a kind of alternation between general and objective information and other more subjective content, which comprises testimonies and snapshots captured by the narrator (Linhart), along with considerations related to the trajectory and development of the investigation. These latter materials (with subjective content and form) as a direct expression of the narration—posed as an *I*—, directly address the reader; they are presented as close-up shots and are juxtaposed to geographic, historical, and social data that function as long shots or products of a long-distance view—in this case, enhancing and mediating, with the value of objectivity and as a driving force behind reflexive subsumption, an understanding of the above mentioned direct and close-up scenes and testimonies.

A keen sense of montage organises the whole, alternating between a close-up view and another from afar and governing connections between sequences, sometimes presented as long continuous shots, other times prompting abrupt diegetic cuts that transport the narrative thread to another temporal or spatial context. Yet, the connecting thread is not lost, since, in such cuts, the reflexive intensity is heightened.

This happens, for example, in the chapter 'Return to Recife', when a tracking shot focusing on the landscape, seen from the windows of a moving car headed for Recife, describes scenes of the plantation's undulating leaves, made up of sugar cane stalks that serially follow one another. Meanwhile, the sea of sugarcane fields is interrupted, here and there, by two kinds of patches (brown areas, traces of fires, and, less frequently, isolated remnants of tropical forests) and also by a third, linear one: red furrows that reveal the bare earth, exposing the pathways for the outflow of production. (In less than half a dozen lines, this sequence of images visually summarises an entire centuries-old history of land ownership, in the form of monoculture latifundia; the nefarious and precarious use of burning as a means of preparing the next harvest; the opening of productive territories through environmental devastation.)

The tracking shot's focus shifts, giving way next to a small "panoramic" turn, leaving the landscape that flowed through the windshield and windows in the form of the images alluded to above, to then move on to the face of the driver, who recites, with a theatrical voice, Ferreira Gullar's poem 'A bomba suja' [The Dirty Bomb], which he knows by heart, and which plays the key role that we have already discussed in the reflexive structuring of *The Sugar and The Hunger*'s account. A diegetic cut then emerges, with the simple introduction of the word "Recife" at the beginning of the next paragraph, in a one-word sentence, equivalent to a photograph or fixed wide shot that divides up the narrative, moving it from the car trip that crossed the rural environment to the entrance to the state capital's urban environment.

The abrupt diegetic cut then gives way to the visual presentation of Professor Nelson Chaves and his library in a modest apartment. In sharp and concise sentences — reproduced with such vividness that they evoke an "immediate" effect of presence —, the interviewee explains the history, scope, and impact of mass hunger on the working population. If the spatial and temporal cut is, in fact, abrupt and *shocks* the reader — contrasting with the previous sequence set within a moving vehicle —, the dialectical unification achieved by the connecting thread overcomes the cut, intensified as it is by the demand for an explanation in the face of the preceding objective and "subjective" situations. These give rise to the succinct and precise explanation provided by the interviewee.

In this way, a scientific discourse intersects with the diegetic contemporaneity (rich in images) of the investigative journey. Malnutrition and the current shortage of food, resulting from the greed of large landowners and the prioritisation of monoculture, are aggravated by the wage compression demanded by the transformation of the sugarcane agroindustry into the ethanol production. The process, which distinguishes diets according to epochs, is periodized by Professor Chaves in historical terms.

"One day it will be known"

The exposition reaches its apex in the story of Linhart's (the narrator) meeting with João Virgínio da Silva, founding member and one of the few survivors of the pre-1964 peasant organisation (despite the various tortures and years of imprisonment he endured under the dictatorship). The narrator's encounter with João Virgínio is recounted with epic simplicity and strength:

Galiléia

"During these days, when the strike was being prepared, I travelled across many *municípios*, going from one union meeting to the next. During one of these sessions, I had an encounter that left a strong impression. I was asking questions to peasants about their living conditions, when a man entered. As he intervened in the discussion everyone suddenly fell silent, in a sign of respect. When he stopped talking they told me: "In front of you is João Virginio da Silva, the founder of the peasant league of Galiléia." He was an old man, dressed in a dark costume, sunglasses. He leaned on a cane. His look, his physiognomy, made me think of one of these old leaders of the Algerian National Liberation Front, that one feels has overcome the wounds, mutilations, sicknesses, to hold out, straight and standing upright, and whose simplicity, and worn elegance, inspires respect. The serious and calm voice of João Virginio da Silva strikes through with natural authority. "I am very glad to meet you," I told him. "What do you think of the present situation in this region?" – "I will only answer you at my place," he tells me."[18]

Thus invited, Linhart goes to João Virgínio's home, located on land expropriated from the latifundium, which witnessed the heroic origins of the Peasant Leagues during Miguel Arraes's first government (1963–64), interrupted by the 1964 coup. The landscape, its memory, and its current state (after the dictatorship's eradication of the physical vestiges of the Leagues), reemerge in the reading also in epic terms, dialectically oscillating between genesis and disappearance.

In this way, the readers do not find themselves facing terms faded and weakened by time. Indeed, even when

The Sugar and The Hunger's narrative adopts, in the conclusion, an introspective and lyrical tone, on a narrative *solo* that juxtaposes ambiguous or uncertain sensations ("a crepuscular state, a still pale morning"), the words set in 1979-80, echo loudly today, in 2023.

"In the midst of the profoundest terror, a resistance has been kept alive among the Brazilian peasantry. Now that the social pressure [19] and the economic crisis have weakened the dictatorship,[20] the features, once again, become visible."

"It is like a crepuscular state, a still pale morning. A landscape emerges from a very black and long night. One glimpses forms one thought were erased. So, everything was there, moving in the darkness, unknown. One day, [21] we will know."[22]

Epic and Reflection

An epic, tragic, and, ultimately, lyrical kind of mural painting, *The Sugar and The Hunger* is indissociable, as we have seen, from the vigour of its visual expression. How to explain this intrinsic connection between aspects that, at first glance, seem heterogeneous? The issue is complex and requires consideration of Linhart's previous work, the extraordinary *The Assembly Line*—a truly cinematic work that, as we read it, seems to unfold, in sound and sight, before our very eyes. Such power to visually evoke also possibly calls for comparison with a similar historical aesthetic paradigm: Eisenstein's epic and intellectual cinema, created under the influence of the October Revolution, before Stalinism's consolidation.[23] However, this question cannot be fully addressed in a supporting text like this, although it strongly bears on this reading.

In fact, *The Sugar and The Hunger* and *The Assembly Line*, which was published shortly before, are connected—not just by the remarkable continuity of the writing process, but also, in a systematic way—by the same political interest in workers' forms of organisation, having as a key point the raising of consciousness and the transition to organised collective action. In both, Robert Linhart achieves such an effective critical-reflexive reach and power of visual evocativeness that it remains difficult, if not impossible, unless I am mistaken, to determine the discursive foundation or aspect that prevails over the whole: the historical-political judgement, the philosophical insight, or the dimension of perception and plastic-imaginary. In short, the synthesis achieved—difficult to obtain in the context of a modern art so inclined toward fragmentation and the primacy of individual sensations—is that of a critical epic order, which—without illusions and beyond all determinism—condenses, in itself, the contradictions and struggles of an era.

Between Epic-Critical Saga and "Fire Alarm"[24]

In summary, *The Sugar and The Hunger* is highly valuable as a document of an era and as a laboratory study attesting to an historical shift in capitalism. The ongoing project of dismantling the welfare state certainly had a crucial moment in the case of Chile, as mentioned earlier. Yet, the same global process of liquidating the rights (of labour and self-organisation) of the working class, and of confiscating basic reproductive goods (self-subsistence and housing) also drew, to some extent, from the ominous experiment in question that took place in the rural areas of the Brazilian *Nordeste*, under the civilian-military dictatorship established from 1964 onwards.

In short, the experiment in question was traced and captured in historical terms fifteen years later by Robert Linhart, examining its development coupled with the expansion of the automotive industry in Brazil (where branches of the giants in the sector, such as Volkswagen and Fiat, achieved a grander scale than that of their headquarters in Germany and Italy). Accordingly, this study not only reveals the violence at the heart of the entire neoliberal experience,[25] but also warns that the devastation to which such a process leads remains incalculable and continues to unfold to this day.

From Regional Experiment to Global Reality

The capitalist economic system today is globalised and unified. Income concentration on a global scale is a systemic reality in the G20 economies, as well as the relative global compression of the wage bill, even though Southeast Asian industrialization has expanded the world working class on a large scale in

absolute numbers. Numbers are unnecessary in the face of
a tendency that anyone can clearly see.

Meanwhile, who does not see that the images of the
tragic migrations of desperate populations—desperate to leave
the *concentration camps* that their homelands have been turned
into—contribute decisively to restraining wage demands
wherever they may arise? As long as capitalism has the energy
and power to globally foment, in strategic locations, its
concentration camps for the global display of the appalling power
of mass hunger and chronic pandemics, the compression of
wages and the concentration of capital will go on; just as "the
immense rotting," as *The Sugar and The Hunger* warns, of
everything and everyone will too.

What else do we have to lose?

I would like to thank Maitê Fanchini for accessing and handling texts and documents from Robert Linhart's archives, which she partly digitised, and for indicating the recent study referred to in note 9.

I also thank Gustavo Motta for his sharp revision and comments.

1   *The Sugar and The Hunger* [*Le Sucre et la Faim: Enquête dans les régions sucrières du Nord-Est brésilien*, Les éditions de Minuit, Paris, 1980], is an extraordinary – yet simple and crystalline – book, which does not require any prior explanations. My afterword deals with subsequent facts and questions.

2   "If we look for the vital element in Brazil's formation, the element that lies at the very roots of its subsequent growth, we will find it in the fact that the colony was established to provide sugar, tobacco, and certain other commodities; later gold and diamonds; then cotton, and later still coffee for the European market. This was the objective in the establishment of the Brazilian economy, an externally oriented objective, turned away from the country itself and taking account of nothing more than the commercial interests involved." Caio Prado Jr., *The Colonial Background of Modern Brazil*, trans. Suzette Macedo, University of California Press, Berkeley, 1967, p. 21. [Braz. orig.: *Formação do Brasil Contemporâneo: Colônia* [1942], São Paulo: Brasiliense/ Publifolha, 2000, p. 20.]

3   The Institutional Act No. 5 (referred to as AI-5), which intensified the repressive power of the civil-military dictatorship, was decreed on December 13, 1968.

4   For a recent review of the critical work and debates provoked by Marxist dependency theory, see Claudio Katz, *La Teoría de la Dependencia, Cincuenta Años Después*, Batalla de Ideas, Buenos Aires, 2018. [*Dependency Theory After Fifty Years: The Continuing Relevance of Latin American Critical Thought*, Haymarket, Chicago, 2023.]

5   See André Gunder Frank, *Reflexiones sobre la Crisis Económica*, trad. Angels Martínez Castells et. al., Editorial Anagrama, Barcelona, 1977. [*Reflections on The World Economic Crisis*, Monthly Review Press, New York, 1981]

6   On the neoliberal experiment in Santiago, Naomi Klein affirms: "Out of this live laboratory emerged the first Chicago School state [Chile], and the first victory in its global counterrevolution." Naomi Klein, *The Shock Doctrine: The Rise of Disaster Capitalism*, Picador, New York, 2007, p. 87.

7   For details on *El Ladrillo*, the economic plan that formed the basis of the experiment, prepared (with funding from the CIA) by a group of Chilean economists from the Universidad Católica (graduates from the University of Chicago and former students of Milton Friedman), see *idem*, pp. 86-87. See also Carola Fuentes and Rafael Valdeavellano's film *Chicago Boys*, digital, colour, Chile, 2015, 85', available at: http://etudoverdade.com.br/br/filme/42087-Chicago-Boys. For a comprehensive and concise assessment of the neoliberal experiment in Chile, later applied in central economies, see N. Klein, op. cit., chapters 1-4, pp. 29-143. For further developments in Italy and central economies, see L. R. Martins, "A era dos genocídios" [The Era of Genocides], September 30, 2021, and "A era dos genocídios–II" [The Era of Genocides–II], October 22, 2021, on the website *A Terra É Redonda*, available respectively at: https://aterraeredonda.com.br/a-era-dos-genocidios/ and https://aterraeredonda.com.br/a-era-dos-genocidios-ii/.

8   Pejorative nickname arising from rushed and cold food, typical of informal labour relations.

9   For the persistence and worsening (according to official reports) of current conditions for "forced labour," in the mould of pro-slavery, see Julien Bouissou and Kenza Soares El Sayed, "Sucre industriel : le spectre du travail forcé/ Des groupes européens s'approvisionnent dans des plantations brésiliennes où seraient bafoués les droits humains" in *Le Monde*/ Économie & Entreprise/ *Enquête*, Paris, Saturday, 31 Dec. 2022-Sunday, 1st–Monday, 2nd Jan. 2023, p. 17.

10 Regarding this topic, see the film by Errol Morris, *The Fog of War* [USA, 2003], an extended interview with former Ford executive (1946) and former US Secretary of Defense (1961-68) Robert McNamara (1916–2009); available at: https://www.youtube.com/watch?v=pu-uwKW_4ys.

11 Just as he had read books in the original Portuguese by the Brazilian writers Graciliano Ramos (1892-1953), Carlos Drummond de Andrade (1902-1987), and Guimarães Rosa (1908-1967), and, of course, those

directly quoted in *The Sugar and The Hunger*. Cf.
testimony collected on 22. IX. 2022. See Robert
Linhart in L.R. Martins, *Conversations With Robert
Linhart*, film, 36 minutes, Brazil, 2023.

12 See Michael Löwy, *Fire Alarm: Reading Walter
Benjamin's 'On the Concept of History'*, translated
by Chris Turner, Verso, London, 2005.

13 See Francisco Julião, *Cambão (Le joug): La Face Cachée
du Brésil*, trad. Anny Meyer, Paris, éd. François
Maspero, 1968, p. 88. [Engl. trans.: *Cambão – The Yoke:
The Hidden Face of Brazil*, trans. John Butt, Penguin,
Harmondsworth, 1972]

14 See Ferreira Gullar, "*A bomba suja*" [1975], in *Dentro
da Noite Veloz* [Inside the Speedy Night] [1975],
pref. Armando Freitas Filho, Companhia das Letras,
São Paulo, 2018.

15 Addressed in the novel *Vidas Secas* (1938), by Graciliano
Ramos (made into a film by Nelson Pereira dos Santos
in 1963), this problem, historically linked to the seasonal
scourge of drought – was converted into a permanent
flow after the aforementioned confiscation of homes.
From the next literary generation, the poem by João
Cabral de Melo Neto, "Morte e Vida Severina [*Life
and Death of a Severino*]/ Auto de Natal Pernambucano
[Christmas Auto from Pernambuco] 1954-1955" (in idem,
Obra Completa [Complete Works], single volume, ed. org.
by Marly de Oliveira with the assistance of the author,
Biblioteca Luso-Brasileira/ Nova Aguilar, Rio de Janeiro,
1999, pp. 169-202), was adapted after 1964 and became
the basis for a university play (1965) with a significant
impact. The play was set to music by Chico Buarque de
Holanda and was also presented, with similar impact, at
the Nancy University Theater Festival (France, 1966).

16 Karl Marx, "Debates on the Thefts of Wood", Karl
Marx and Friedrich Engels, *Collected Works*, Volume 1,
Lawrence & Wishart, London, 1975.

17 R. Linhart, *Le Sucre et la Faim*, p. 62. *The Sugar and the
Hunger*, p. 91 [In this book].

18 R. Linhart, *op. cit.*, pp. 85-86. *The Sugar and the
Hunger*, p. 124-25 [In this book].

19 Allusion to the wave of great strikes by metallurgists, which broke out in the industrial centre of the ABC, in the state of São Paulo, from 1978 onwards, and which gave rise, in 1980, to the founding of the Workers' Party .

20 Possible allusion to the political amnesty law, enacted by the regime in August 1979. Thanks to it, Miguel Arraes was able to return to Brazil, and by extension invite (as translator of the Brazilian edition of *L'Établi. Greve na Fábrica* [1978, Paz e Terra]) Robert Linhart to visit the country, a trip that is at the origin of the investigation that resulted in *The Sugar and The Hunger*.

21 *October 30, 2022*, it would seem that the day in question (alluded to in the final line of *The Sugar and The Hunger*) has arrived – if not entirely, then at least casting some preparatory lights. Thus, with *all* the other regions in Brazil having sanctioned the reelection of the ultraright faction within the national government, it was the votes from the *Nordeste* (by a large majority, on average, of two thirds, but sometimes as much as three quarters, against the government), in addition to the female vote, that were responsible – principally and directly – for halting the growth of the ultraright within the country. The composition of votes in the *Nordeste* was also significant, from the standpoint of the country's social and political structure, as it overturned a cliché established at the end of the dictatorship and the transition to the so-called *Nova República*, when it was thought that the "progressive" votes came mainly from the urban centres of the South-East and South, leaving the *Nordestino* and rural electorate, inversely, under the control of oligarchies. This time, the votes in the Southeast gave way, by a slim majority – though sometimes even an ample one (in the South) – to the advance of the ultraright.

22 R. Linhart, *op. cit.*, p. 93. *The Sugar and the Hunger*, p. 133 [In this book].

23 As a contemporary of Linhart's writings, the epic-documentary and investigative cinema of the Argentine director Fernando 'Pino' Solanas (1936–2020) would also call for such a comparison.

24 I draw here on Michael Löwy's expression, used as the title of his book (see note 12 above).

25 For a detailed comparative discussion of the controversy surrounding the origins of neoliberalism as a new "normative logic" in the wake of Michel Foucault's political vision, tributary to the so-called "*deuxième gauche,*" and of the views of those who, in contrast, see the emergence of neoliberalism as indissolubly linked to violence, see L. R. Martins, "A era dos genocides", op. cit. (see note 7 above).

Robert Linhart

The Sugar and the Hunger
An Inquiry into the Sugar Regions of Northeastern Brazil

(Le Sucre et la Faim: Enquête dans les régions sucrières
du Nord-Est brésilien)

Edited by
Sezgin Boynik

Afterword
Luiz Renato Martins

Translation
John M Floyd (Linhart)
Emillio Sauri (Renato Martins)

Proofreading
Elizabeth Dexter

Graphic Design
Ott Kagovere

Typeface
Turist by Andree Paat
(Typokompanii)

Thank you
Rodrigo Almeida
Jean Copans
Maitê Fanchini
Mark Foss
Johannes Fridholm
Carmela Gross
François Manceaux
Luiz Renato Martins
Minus Miele
Gustavo Motta
Patrick Ruth

Printed in
Tallinn Book Printers